DESIGN
THINKING

for *School Leaders*

Five Roles and Mindsets That
Ignite Positive Change

ASCD MEMBER BOOK

Many ASCD members received this book as a
member benefit upon its initial release.

Learn more at: **www.ascd.org/memberbooks**

DESIGN THINKING

for *School Leaders*

Five Roles and Mindsets That Ignite Positive Change

Alyssa **Gallagher**

Kami **Thordarson**

Alexandria, Virginia USA

1703 N. Beauregard St. • Alexandria, VA 22311-1714 USA
Phone: 800-933-2723 or 703-578-9600 • Fax: 703-575-5400

Website: www.ascd.org • E-mail: member@ascd.org
Author guidelines: www.ascd.org/write

Deborah S. Delisle, *Executive Director;* Stefani Roth, *Publisher;* Genny Ostertag, *Director, Content Acquisitions;* Susan Hills, *Acquisitions Editor;* Julie Houtz, *Director, Book Editing & Production;* Joy Scott Ressler, *Editor;* Thomas Lytle, *Graphic Designer;* Mike Kalyan, *Director, Production Services;* Kyle Steichen, *Production Specialist;* Keith Demmons, *Production Designer.*

Portions of the text are from the authors' blog.

All web links in this book are correct as of the publication date below but may have become inactive or otherwise modified since that time. If you notice a deactivated or changed link, please e-mail books@ascd.org with the words "Link Update" in the subject line. In your message, please specify the web link, the book title, and the page number on which the link appears.

PAPERBACK ISBN: 978-1-4166-2594-0   ASCD product #118022

PDF E-BOOK ISBN: 978-1-4166-2596-4; see Books in Print for other formats.

Quantity discounts are available: e-mail programteam@ascd.org or call 800-933-2723, ext. 5773, or 703-575-5773. For desk copies, go to www.ascd.org/deskcopy.

ASCD Member Book No. FY18-7 (May 2018 P). ASCD Member Books mail to Premium (P), Select (S), and Institutional Plus (I+) members on this schedule: Jan, PSI+; Feb, P; Apr, PSI+; May, P; Jul, PSI+; Aug, P; Sep, PSI+; Nov, PSI+; Dec, P. For current details on membership, see www.ascd.org/membership.

Library of Congress Cataloging-in-Publication Data is available for this title.
Names: Gallagher, Alyssa, author. | Thordarson, Kami.
Title: Design thinking for school leaders : five roles and mindsets that
    ignite positive change / Alyssa Gallagher and Kami Thordarson.
Description: Alexandria, Va. : ASCD, 2018. | Includes bibliographical
    references and index.
Identifiers: LCCN 2018003588 (print) | LCCN 2018013513 (ebook) | ISBN
    9781416625964 (PDF) | ISBN 9781416625940 (pbk.)
Subjects: LCSH: Educational leadership–United States. | Educational
    change–United States. | School management and organization–United States.
Classification: LCC LB2805 (ebook) | LCC LB2805 .G25 2018 (print) | DDC
    371.2/011–dc23
LC record available at https://lccn.loc.gov/2018003588

26 25 24 23 22 21 20 19 18   2 3 4 5 6 7 8 9 10 11 12

DESIGN THINKING
for *School Leaders*

Five Roles and Mindsets That Ignite Positive Change

Chapter 1

Design-Inspired Leadership

A leader takes people where they want to go. A great leader takes people where they don't necessarily want to go, but ought to be.

—Rosalynn Carter, former First Lady

A Call to Action

It's no secret: schools need to change. Everywhere you go, educators are talking about change. Whether at educational conferences, school district meetings, or in school hallways, there are many discussions about the need for education to be different. Sometimes it feels as if we are living in an echo chamber, with everyone talking about and even agreeing that change needs to happen, but most are unsure where to start. In many places, a "culture of powerlessness" has been accepted as the status quo. Teachers and site leaders feel bound by habits, traditions, and test scores, mostly because our current school system is designed around two primary design principles, both of which are outdated:

1. Students come to school as empty vessels or blank slates ready to have their heads filled with knowledge.
2. This is best accomplished in an assembly-line format in which students are batched and grouped to proceed through a fixed amount of knowledge to prepare them for their futures.

These two design principles served us well for many years, but are no longer sufficient. In a VUCA—Volatile, Uncertain, Chaotic, Ambiguous—world, what does it mean to prepare our kids for their futures? Are we learning as fast as our world is changing? If not, why not? Now, more than ever, school leaders, both in classrooms and administrative offices, are needed to move us beyond the conversation about change and start *making* changes.

So how do we move beyond the talk?

Portrait of a School Leader

School leaders have historically been portrayed fairly negatively in the media. From *Ferris Bueller's Day Off* to the HBO series *Vice Principals*, school leaders are almost always inane characters or ineffective managers at best who care more about the rules and procedures than the actual well-being or education of students at their schools. While those portrayals may not be accurate, they do highlight the traditional view of "principal as manager," a role that no longer captures the complexity of school leadership. And while it is easy to laugh at the ways in which principals are portrayed, sadly, the role of the principal hasn't evolved as much as the world around it. This failure to morph the principal into a more modern leadership role may be one of the reasons for such a high turnover rate. Annually, there is a 20 percent turnover rate among public school principals. Year after year, approximately 12 percent of all school principals leave the profession, either to retirement or other careers, and 8 percent move on to other roles within education. This number is only slightly lower in private schools (Goldring & Taie, 2014). And sadly, turnover is much worse in troubled schools, where every year, nearly 30 percent of principals quit and, by year three, more than half of all principals leave their jobs. We can't help but wonder if all this transition is partly due to dissatisfaction with the role of school principal.

Unfortunately, the high turnover rate is not only limited to school principal roles; it applies to teachers as well. In the past, it was common to celebrate teachers' retirements representing 25 to 35 years of teaching. Nowadays, it is a much different picture. In the last 15 years, the turnover rate has increased, with teachers leaving the classroom for alternative careers in educational technology or leaving the field of education altogether. Studies from the U.S. Department of Education show that 17 percent of teachers who entered the field in 2007–2008 left the profession within the first five years. Teacher leaders are an important key to creating the change that is needed, not only because changes are needed in the classroom, but also because we need a qualified leadership pipeline for the future. What if there were more or different opportunities for teacher leaders? Could we create a new profile of the school leader that is more effective and therefore more appealing?

Disruption

The world is changing rapidly. Our learners have changed, and everything in the world of education must change, as well. We are in the middle of major disruptions in almost every industry (see Figure 1.1), including learning, yet our roles and infrastructures haven't kept up. Learning has been disrupted by technology, which has altered how we learn. For the first time in history, people of all ages can learn anything they want at any time of day with little more than a device and an Internet connection.

For example, making the news in Ohio, an 8-year-old decided he was hungry, but both parents were fast asleep in the house.

He had seen his parents drive their car and decided the best way to quickly learn was to watch videos on YouTube. After viewing what he felt was enough instruction, he and his younger sister ventured out to McDonald's . . . in their parents' car! While it was a short distance to travel, he apparently followed every rule of the road and handled the vehicle without incident. Imagine the surprise of the McDonald's worker when an 8-year-old expertly pulled up to the drive-thru window. Learning has changed.

Figure 1.1

Disruption

A few indicators of global change:

- The world's biggest taxi company does not own any taxis (Uber).
- One of the largest accommodation providers owns no real estate (Airbnb).
- What has become one of the most popular media sites creates no content (Facebook).
- The world's largest movie provider owns no cinemas (Netflix).
- Two of the largest software vendors don't write their apps (Apple and Google).

Source: From "The Battle Is for the Customer Interface," by T. Goodwin, 2015, TechCrunch. Retrieved from https://techcrunch.com/2015/03/03/in-the-age-of-disintermediation-the-battle-is-all-for-the-customer-interface/.

The World Economic Forum, a nonprofit organization established in 1971, engages political, business, and societal leaders in discussions around the many issues facing our world. One of their primary concerns is education, because they don't see education broadly making the changes necessary to keep up with how fast the rest of the world is evolving.

"We are today at the beginning of a Fourth Industrial Revolution. Developments in previously disjointed fields, such as artificial intelligence and machine learning, robotics, nanotechnology, 3D printing, and genetics and biotechnology are all building on and amplifying one another. Smart systems—homes, factories, farms, grids, or entire cities—will help tackle problems ranging from supply-chain management to climate change" (World Economic Forum, 2016b, p. 1).

With the world changing so quickly, how can we get to a place where schools are experimenting and able to adapt at the rate needed to keep up? We are in the middle of major disruptions that are requiring new abilities and roles in our future workplaces. Innovation is pushing us to fine-tune our skills in data collection and interpretation and demanding that we master lifelong learning. With the rate of change increasing exponentially, leadership will also need to draw on new strategies and practices to work with and support new talent, the younger population of educators who are more adaptable and accustomed to a change-oriented environment. The skills to manage, shape, and lead the changes underway will be in short supply unless we take action today to develop them. "For a talent revolution to take place, governments and businesses will need to profoundly change their approach to education, skills, and employment, and their approach to working with each other" (World Economic Forum, 2016b, p. 7).

The role of school leaders—whether the principal or the head of school—needs a major disruption, too. What if leaders were able to approach their work more like designers? Designers actually see the world differently and therefore bring a new perspective to their work. This new perspective is desperately needed in schools and really does begin with the school leader. We call this new perspective *design-inspired leadership* and believe it is one of the most powerful ways to spark positive change and address education challenges using the same design and innovation principles that have been so successful in private industry.

Design-Inspired Leadership

The word "design" can be elusive to define; however, we know it when we see it. We certainly know when we experience poor design, because it usually means that something isn't working.

In a blog post on experience mapping by Jared Spool (n.d.) we came across this definition of design:

"Design is the rendering of intent (para. 7)."

A designer works to make their intentions real in the world. Regardless of our background and experience, educators are all actually designers with the common goal of making education better. Design might happen unintentionally, but it happens. From the principal planning next week's staff meeting, to the creation of school goals, implementation of new programs, and the meeting of new mandates, we are constantly designing. Without taking the time to understand design principles, many leaders are operating as "accidental designers," occasionally stumbling upon innovative ideas or solutions. With more background on design, we believe we can help leaders shift from "accidental designers" to "design-inspired leaders," acting with greater intention and achieving greater impact.

Design-inspired leadership deals with more than just process; it is rooted in mindsets that you adopt in your work. Approaching Design Thinking as just a process can reduce it to a series of meetings and checklists. Design-driven leadership offers opportunities for moments of impact, often unscripted and unplanned but still intentional, and the mindsets are what help you identify these opportunities. These mindsets correspond to the five roles of leaders embedded within design-inspired leadership (see Figure 1.2), which will help you move from an accidental designer to an intentional designer—one who embraces an explorer's mindset, ready to discover something new rather than return to something familiar. Intentional designers in education will need tools for creating real, lasting, and replicable change in their schools and districts.

Design-inspired leadership is a shift from the traditional view or role; it is a dramatic move away from *Leader as Manager* and a move toward *Leader as Designer*. Figure 1.3 outlines traits of both traditional leadership and design-inspired leadership.

Figure 1.2

Roles Embedded Within Design-Inspired Leadership

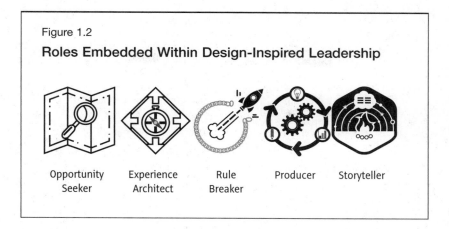

| Opportunity Seeker | Experience Architect | Rule Breaker | Producer | Storyteller |

Which column inspires you more? What type of leader do you want to work for? What type of leader do you want to be?

This book is for school leaders who understand the need to lead differently, but could use some practical help in imagining a new role, both what it looks like and how to get there. Written with a clear goal in mind, this book will put you in the driver's seat and enable you to make choices about both the pace of change and the distance you wish to travel. Even if you only engage with a few of the strategies partway, we believe they will result in positive changes for your school. We will reframe the role of a school leader by sharing five new roles and tools to develop the skills necessary to make these changes. Each of these five roles includes a set of stances and mindsets. Some roles may feel very familiar in your work, while others may be new. While the outcomes of design-inspired leadership can be dramatic, the steps you take don't need to be. The change to this new way of leading can be accomplished with a series of small steps that build over time into big wins.

We will explore the following five roles in this book:

1. *Opportunity Seeker.* Shifts from problem solving to problem finding and actively seeking opportunities.

Figure 1.3

Traditional Leadership Versus Design-Inspired Leadership

Traditional Leadership	Design-Inspired Leadership
• Leader (teacher) centered	• User (student) centered
• Heavily influenced by organizational hierarchy and time in the role	• Recognizes the intelligence in the room regardless of "status" within the organization
• Afraid to venture beyond what has been strictly deemed "best practices"	• Not afraid to go beyond "best practices" to experiment with new solutions
• Yes, but, or no	
• Begins with constraints	• Begins with possibilities. Leads with "What if . . . ?"
• Slow to act	
• Starts with answers	• Bias toward action
• Fearful of unknown	• Starts with questions
• Prefers things to fit in their boxes	• Embraces ambiguity
• Takes the safe path	• Comfortable with the messiness of learning
• Values being right and risks avoidance	• Values great questions and experimentation
• Fixed mindset	• Growth mindset

2. *Experience Architect.* Designs and curates learning experiences based on needs that stretch the current status quo.
3. *Rule Breaker.* Thoughtfully challenges the way things are "always" done.
4. *Producer.* Hustles, gets things done, creates rapid learning cycles for his or her teams, and is responsible for shipping a "final" product.
5. *Storyteller.* Captures the hearts and minds of a community to amplify the good and create authentic community.

These new roles will help school leaders realize both their true potential and the true potential of their organizations. We are at the forefront of the design + education movement.

Design Thinking

Everything in modern society is the result of a collection of decisions made by someone. Why shouldn't that someone be you?

—Tom Kelley, *Creative Confidence: Unleashing the Creative Potential Within Us All*

Before we dive into reimagining the principal role, it will be helpful to have a basic understanding of Design Thinking and some foundational design principles. Design Thinking isn't unknown in the educational space. In recent years, interest in Design Thinking has grown among educators as it is a natural complement to inquiry, project-based learning, collaboration, and problem solving. Increasingly, teachers are being trained in how to use Design Thinking as a means to promote student creativity and problem solving. In fact, you can join a community of teachers having weekly conversations about Design Thinking in the classroom by using #dtk12chat on Twitter every Wednesday night. There are three primary ways we see Design Thinking being used in education today:

1. As a pedagogical tool (essentially teaching students to be design thinkers)
2. As a tool for teachers to design learning experiences
3. As a tool for school leaders to design school change

While the awareness of Design Thinking is growing among teachers, less attention has been paid to how leading like a designer can influence both the rate and type of changes being made in education.

Design Thinking is a process for problem solving and a method for creative action whose origins date back to the 1960s, when design methods and practices were being investigated as a way to solve "wicked problems." "Wicked problems are those that are difficult or impossible to solve because of incomplete, contradictory, and changing requirements that are challenging to recognize"

(Wicked problem, n.d., para. 1). Think of global warming or world hunger. In education, think of personalized learning, closing the achievement gap, or meeting the needs of second-language learners. Design Thinking began moving into the business world in two major areas: companies using the design process to create innovative products, and companies using the design process to rethink their current methods and models of operation.

We begin with the process, because it is in the process that the mindsets of designers come to life. Figure 1.4 is an example based on one of the most well-known design thinking processes from the Stanford d.school.

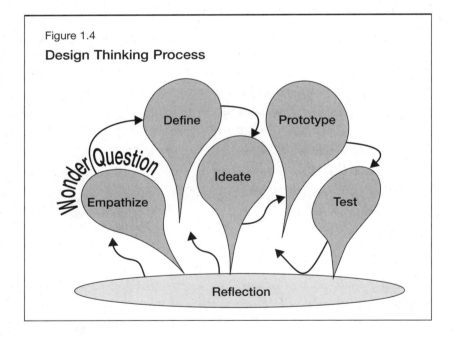

Figure 1.4
Design Thinking Process

To help you better understand Design Thinking, Figure 1.5 outlines the purpose of each stage in the design thinking process, design thinking mindsets, and helpful tips to keep in mind. While this overview only touches the surface of Design Thinking, it will help you understand the foundation from which we are building. We encourage you to jump in and play. Design Thinking

Figure 1.5

Design Thinking Process, Mindsets, and Helpful Tips

Wonder and Question	Mindfulness is becoming an important component to our lives. Part of wondering and questioning is to become aware of your own identity, values, emotions, biases, and assumptions that you may be carrying into the process.
	Ask, "How might my perceptions and assumptions influence my thinking?"
	Helpful tips:
	• List everything you think or think you might know about the person or situation you're designing for.
	• Reflect on where your bias may be showing and ask where your knowledge or full understanding may be lacking.
	• What new wonders and questions do you have?
Empathize	Learn about the audience for which you are designing.
	Ask, "Who is my user?" "What is important to this person?"
	Helpful tips:
	• Three quick ways to develop empathy are observation, interview, and immersion. The art of empathetic observation is a means to observe and listen to our users as they teach and learn. It's like looking over their shoulders while trying to imagine what they are thinking and feeling. The empathy interview is an approach to finding out as much as possible about a person's experience as the user of a space, a process, an objective, or an environment. Immersion is your most powerful tool for achieving empathy, as it allows you to enter the world of your users. In schools, this means shadowing a student or teacher for the day.
	• When designing for a large group, identify your extreme users and design to the edges. List a number of facets to explore within your design space, then think of people who may be extreme in those facets. This helps you pull out meaningful needs that may not pop when engaging with the middle of the bell curve. Pay special attention to work-arounds (or other extreme behaviors) that can serve as inspiration and uncover insights.

continued

Figure 1.5 (*continued*)

Design Thinking Process, Mindsets, and Helpful Tips

Define	Create a point of view that is based on user needs and insights.
	Ask, "What are their needs?"
	Helpful tips:
	• Clarity at this stage can lead to more relevant solutions. Move beyond what seems to be the apparent need and dig deep. What are we really solving? If you don't have as much clarity as you want at an early stage, remember that while some problems are defined for us, others may be discovered in the design process.
Ideate	Brainstorm and come up with as many creative solutions as possible.
	Ask crazy questions to prompt thinking. *"How would I solve this problem if I had $1 million?" "How would Walt Disney solve this problem?"*
	Helpful tips:
	• Good ideating takes a page from improv. Try "yes, and . . ." not "yes, but . . . "
	• Don't limit yourself; go for quantity!
Prototype	Build a representation of one or more of your ideas to show others.
	Ask, "How can I show my idea?" "What does a rough draft of this idea look like?"
	Helpful tips:
	• Don't fall in love with your idea; our first ideas are usually our worst! Get feedback quickly to keep your relationship with your idea healthy.
	• You can use anything as prototyping materials—remember, you are just building to learn.

Test	Share a prototyped idea with your original use for feedback. Ask, "What worked?" "What didn't?" "What can be improved?" **Helpful tips:** • Encourage honest feedback. • Poor designs are often the result of not spending enough time in the testing phase. Cycle back and forth between prototyping and testing as many times as needed.
Reflection	Reflection is an ongoing process throughout the design thinking process. Ask, "What evidence do we have that we are self-aware and self-correcting as we move through the process?" **Helpful tips:** • Include time for reflection at various points in your process. (Take a selfie!) • Don't forget to check in on the emotional state of your team. Is it impacting the work? • Build in time to connect and release frustrations.

embraces a bias toward action, and the process can easily be applied anywhere in your life. Not ready to experiment at work? Then test out the process with a problem at home. Either way, the reference tool will be helpful as you learn to navigate the design process for yourself. And remember, the only way to get better at Design Thinking is to engage in the messiness of it.

Another version of the design process, which was created by IDEO, one of the most well-known design firms, is "Inspiration, Ideation, and Implementation." As described on IDEO.com, "Inspiration is the problem or opportunity that motivates the search for solutions. Ideation is the process of generating, developing, and testing ideas. Implementation is the path that leads from the project stage into people's lives" (Design Thinking, n.d.).

The exact design thinking process is less important than the core components and mindsets embedded in the process. All design processes share the same foundational components of design (Ertel & Solomon, 2014):

- *Developing* a deep understanding of and empathy for users and their needs.
- *Cycling* through periods of divergent thinking to explore diverse sources of inspiration.
- *Learning* through quick cycles of prototyping, gathering feedback, and making necessary adaptations.
- *Testing* solutions with a small group and only scaling up after they have proved effective in meeting the identified needs.

Design Thinking is messy and nonlinear, which can make it challenging for educators to embrace. Its open-endedness can feel counterintuitive in a world that is often driven by mandates, accountability, top-down decisions, and rigid rules. And yet, as we start to imagine new models of education, design might be just the tool to help overcome common obstacles and resistance to change. Design Thinking empowers all leaders and teachers. It can be a catalyst for changing the culture of powerlessness that exists in many schools today. In times of increasing complexity and constraints, it may be more important than ever for educational leaders to lead like designers. The more you engage in the process, the more comfortable and adept you will feel at adapting it to your specific needs and context.

We encourage you to learn more about Design Thinking by taking a free 90-minute virtual crash course via the Stanford d.school. Not everyone can make the trip to the Stanford d.school. to experience how they teach Design Thinking, but this online tutorial (https://dschool.stanford.edu/resources-collections/a-virtual-crash-course-in-design-thinking) will take you step by step through the process of participating in a 90-minute design challenge.

Getting from the Schools We Have to the Schools We Want

We may not currently have the schools we want, but we can take active steps to shift in that direction. First, we may have to allow ourselves to dream. Do we even know what type of schools we want to create? What if leaders were encouraged to dream big and then able to leverage resources to accomplish those dreams? Google has created a way to make this happen through "Moonshot Thinking," a term used for their most innovative projects, such as the driverless car and augmented reality glasses. "Google simply defines a moonshot project as one that addresses a huge problem, proposes a radical solution, and uses breakthrough technology. Instead of a mere 10 percent gain, a moonshot aims for a 10x improvement over what currently exists. The combination of a huge problem, a radical solution to that problem, and the break-through technology that just might make that solution possible, is the essence of a moonshot" (X, moonshot factory, 2013).

What if we encouraged school leaders to identify their "moonshot"? What would be on your list? Struggling to identify your moonshot? What if you approached it from another direc-tion? Try listing the top 10 changes you would make to improve student learning if you weren't afraid, and why these changes are important. Would you change how we define homework? Would you change your schedule? If you feel even more daring, share your top 10 with your superintendent, president of the teachers' association, or members of the school board. You are guaran-teed to have some interesting conversations!

Myths About Educational Change

To get closer to our moonshot, we must first revisit and question long-held assumptions. In our work with school leaders, we have uncovered a set of beliefs about change that are really myths. On a rational level, we know that these myths aren't true, and yet we have a tendency to buy into them, even repeating mantras that reinforce these beliefs, without questioning the assumptions behind them. Following are some of the most common myths about educational change we have encountered.

Myth #1: All you need to do is take a monumental leap.

Reality: In most cases, a leap is a result of lots of tinkering behind the scenes. Yes, there may be a radical jump within an organization, but there has likely been a series of shifts and small movements happening that helped pave the way for the big leap. Our organizational systems in education are slow to react, and often "taking a leap" can appear overwhelming and actually shut down big ideas for change. Think about getting your body to jump over or up onto something. Your sensory system and your motor system need to be seamless; biomechanics are at work as every muscle and joint needs to cooperate, and you need momentum. If you spend much of your time on a couch, or your exercise routine does not involve jumping, your first leap may be very small and may leave you on the ground. You can return to the couch, or you can continue to work on all the elements to make the leap in small movements over time.

Myth #2: Even if a leader wants change, there is not enough time, help, or buy-in from others.

Reality: In our world of abundance, we often work from a scarcity perspective. Our first human instinct is to look around and worry about what we don't have. When you get your team together and create time to dig deep into their needs, many of them find themselves in the same worried mindset. Acknowledging these feelings of scarcity and fear can help identify the constraints so that they can be dealt with. You can't help building an abundance of support and camaraderie when you realize you are all in the same boat. The focus shifts from "The boat is leaking and drifting farther from the shore and I don't know how to swim!" to "How can we work together with what we do have to get everyone safely to shore?" It also helps to be clear with your language. For example, replace "I don't have time" with "This isn't a priority." You might be surprised at how quickly this subtle shift can help you get clear on your priorities—we find the time when things are important. It's easy to say that we don't have time to go to the doctor, but when we shift it to "My health isn't a priority," it helps us see how silly our use of time can be. Knowing, understanding, and defining your constraints can lead you to truly creative solutions that shape change.

Myth #3: Change must begin at the top.

Reality: It can be tempting to sit back and wait for someone farther up the food chain to initiate change, but ordinary people who want to see things done initiate many incredible changes. It can be helpful for change to be supported from the top, but it doesn't have to start there. Change can start from the bottom, from grassroots efforts and groups or people who want to see things done differently. One of the benefits of grassroots change in education is that the work happens closer to the students we are trying to impact, and results may be easier to see in a shorter timeframe.

Myth #4: Technology drives innovation.

Reality: Many districts believe that rolling Chromebook or iPad carts into classrooms will instantly move everyone into 21st century teaching and learning. The focus is often on the tools, both hardware and software. We are so anxious to get technology into classrooms that we forget to step back and have a discussion about how it impacts learning. With the addition of technology, you see many students sitting with headphones, working through a playlist of plug-and-play programs or curriculums that are a substitute for textbook learning. The technology has not innovated the practice of teaching and learning; it's just substituted a computer for a pencil and paper. It may be different, but perhaps not better. Invention is the fun part of innovation, but it doesn't always lead to true innovation. As Peter Denning and Robert Dunham describe in their book *The Innovator's Way,* innovation equals "new practices adopted by a community that produces better results" (The Innovator's Way, 2010). This simple distinction opens new insights into how to foster innovation. Reframing innovation as a personal skill means that it is something that can be developed through practice and extended into organizations. So, to put it simply, technology does not equal innovation.

Myth #5: There is a clear path forward and a simple answer that will fix education.

Reality: If only this were true. Broadly speaking, the educational community has been in search of simple and seemingly magical solutions to our complicated problems for years, but sadly, there is no silver bullet. It would be fantastic if there were a manual for change. Whenever you hit a snag, you could simply look it up in the index, turn to that page, and easily find your solution, with the next step clearly defined. That is not the case, because change is messy. Emotions are involved. Habits need to be examined and broken. There is no one right way or linear process that will move your organization forward. We are humans teaching humans, which means all our beliefs and values are wrapped up in our practices. It takes time and empathy to work through different viewpoints and create a new way of thinking about our students, our practices, our classrooms, and our schools.

Assumptions drive our behaviors; therefore, a first step in changing behaviors is to identify the underlying assumptions. What are your assumptions about change in education? What assumptions do your teachers hold? We have provided five common assumptions or myths as a starting point. See if you can identify and bust the most common myths held in your community.

Theory of Change

We believe that educators can solve the challenges that face our schools faster and more effectively than any policy, top-down mandate, or expensive commercial solution. While the education space may not be widely known as a lucrative space for innovation (yet!), we believe it will be, and that this innovation will be driven by educators who are leading like designers. These are educators who are embracing the mindsets and stances of Design Thinking, operating as Opportunity Seekers, Experience Architects, Rule Breakers, Producers, and Storytellers.

We believe that

- *Shifting beliefs is always harder than shifting actions.* People need time to grieve over things that they might be letting go. Find ways to support people in this process and meet them where they are.
- *Change is scary.* It can be challenging for people to unlearn habits and routines that have worked well for them and to connect to a need for change.
- *Top-down change takes away all the voice and choice of our adult learners.* We need innovative change to bubble up. Teachers and leaders must be empowered to come to solutions from a human-centered design process. We want and need to allow teachers to feel what it is like to be a part of the student experience and to honor their insights.
- *Culture is an essential component to the change process.* For sustainable change to take place, there must be a culture of trust and risk taking, where open dialogue is valued and encouraged.
- *Transparency and collaboration are critical.* Invite teachers, parents, and students in behind the curtain. Together, we will be more effective in our problem solving.
- *Life is lived in perpetual beta.* Change is the only constant, and we must decide to disrupt ourselves.
- *Fun is a crucial component of the change process.* Just like students, adults retain more and have more sustainability for what they are working on when they enjoy the process.

So let's begin this journey that will take you from "Leader as Manager" to "Leader as Designer."

Chapter 2

Empathy Is King

*The main tenet of Design Thinking is empathy for the people
you're trying to design for. Leadership is exactly the same thing—
building empathy for the people you're entrusted to help.*

—David Kelley, co-founder of IDEO and author of
Creative Confidence

Empathy is a word that seems to be popping up everywhere. It
has become a buzzword among politicians, education experts,
and business leaders. But what does it really mean? "Empathy
is the ability to share another person's feelings and emotions as
if they were your own" (Collins English Dictionary, n.d.). Empathy
is king in Design Thinking, which differentiates it from many
approaches that are also used to tackle problems. Some people
may be naturally more empathetic, but empathy is a skill that
can and should be practiced. In fact, we believe empathy is one
of the most important skills you can develop on this journey.
Having empathy improves your leadership, teaches you to ask
the right questions, and enables you to understand others better.

Empathy must be the driving force behind changes made in our schools. To effectively move our organizations forward, we must be willing to listen, compromise, and meet people where they are. Empathy allows for honest and transparent communication, which can be both frustrating and uncomfortable. Keep in mind that, while they are close cousins, empathy is not sympathy. Sympathy is more of a third-person emotional response; empathy involves putting yourself in another person's shoes. Think for a moment about the last time someone shared a problem with you. What was your reaction? Did you try to lighten the mood or immediately solve the problem? If so, you might be suffering from a lack of empathy.

A few winters back, you may have read or heard about a New York City police officer who very generously donated a new pair of warm boots to a homeless man sitting on the streets on a particularly cold night. The story went viral after a tourist snapped a picture of the generous donation in action that captured our hearts. What the picture and the story don't tell is what happened next. A *New York Times* reporter tracked down the homeless man, Jeffrey Hamilton, a military veteran who had worked in kitchens before living on the street, and discovered that he was still wandering the streets barefoot. When asked about the footwear, Jeffrey told the reporter he had to hide those expensive boots because they could cost him his life. A heartbreaking story in many regards, we feel that this tale also highlights what happens in education: we supply the solution we think people need or the solution we want them to have, without enough empathy for their needs. We wonder if, had the well-intentioned officer spent more time with Jeffrey, he might have learned about other ways to meet that need, or if Jeffrey had more important needs to be met. In Jeffrey's case, a few layers of socks or a well-worn pair of used boots may have been a better match for his needs. So how do you become more empathetic and uncover the needs of students, teachers, and parents in your community?

How Empathetic Are You?

The latest neuroscience research shows that 98 percent of us have the ability to empathize hardwired into our brains, and yet many of us do not utilize the skill enough. Think of empathy as a muscle. Like any muscle, empathy can be developed over time with intentional practice. The more we have learned about empathy, the more curious we have become. We started wondering how strong our empathetic skills were. If you, too, find yourself wondering, you can take a short quiz that will give you some baseline information. The Empathy Quiz from Greater Good Magazine (http://greatergood.berkeley.edu/quizzes/take_quiz/14) offers a great starting point and draws from three different scientifically validated scales created by researchers to measure empathy. It only takes five minutes to complete, and then you are immediately given both an empathy score and suggestions to help you become more empathetic.

Early in Alyssa's career, she learned about the power of empathy. She became the principal of a highly successful elementary school, as measured by test scores, which was steeped in traditional practices and well versed in "the way we have always done things." There were many clear opportunities to improve student learning, but rather than force her ideas on teachers, she made time to meet with each teacher, gauge their feelings about the school, and talk about how they could collaboratively improve learning for students. Together, they slowly started creating new pathways for success. They identified the need for students to have increased opportunities for highly differentiated learning in both reading and math, which opened the door for student groupings beyond an individual classroom. They also identified a need to embrace passion in learning and saw an opportunity to play with elementary electives and student choice. While there was not an immediate turnaround in everyone's thinking or practice, they made progress toward revolutionizing learning at their school. They continued talking about changes that needed to be made and intentionally provided outlets for everyone to express their thoughts, especially when they disagreed. Outlets for conversation included simple things like an open 15 minutes on a staff meeting agenda or a monthly happy hour when people could connect and share. Opening the door for empathy allows us to engage each other in new ideas and build stronger relationships with those for whom we need to impact change. Because empathy is a skill that actually grows when practiced, the rest of this chapter will focus on concrete ways you can build that empathy muscle.

The Power of Observation

The real act of discovery consists not in finding new lands, but in seeing with new eyes.

—Marcel Proust

One of the first ways to build empathy is to hone your powers of observation and cultivate the ability to see what others overlook. You will be amazed at how much detail actually escapes us on a daily basis. Being able to screen out some detail is important for self-preservation, but imagine if you were able to turn on your observation superpowers when needed.

In 1994, Proctor & Gamble was interested in creating new cleaning solutions. They put together a team that used human-centered design as the primary driver behind any new products. The team, focused on improving the mopping experience, did something very simple and very boring: for hours and hours, they watched people mop. With so many hours of mopping observation, they started to take note of some interesting details. They noticed that mopping was an inherently dirty job, and almost everyone changed their clothes before mopping. They also noticed that mopping was time-consuming, because it was most effective with clean water. If you didn't change the water frequently enough, you were simply smearing around the grime with dirty water. These details started to help frame the true need Proctor & Gamble was trying to fulfill. Then, on one visit with an elderly test subject, coffee grounds were spilled and, instead of reaching for a mop, the woman swept up the grounds and grabbed a damp paper towel to clean up the rest. It was at that moment that the idea for the Swiffer mop was born. Through hours and hours of observation, they discovered a solution that would attract dirt in a one-and-done method. Mopping would no longer be a dirty job and, even better for Procter & Gamble, the Swiffer required ongoing purchases from consumers.

Dev Patnaik, CEO of Jump Associates, a strategy and innovation firm, says, "The secret to good observation is to observe, get bored, and then observe some more" (Patnaik & Mortensen, 2009). If you are like most people, your first response is probably something along the lines of, "Who has time for this? You must be joking!" We both felt this way when we took an online class, "A Crash Course in Creativity," taught by Tina Seelig, a professor at Stanford. Only two weeks into class, we were assigned to take a silent 30-minute walk while observing our surroundings. Alyssa had grand plans for how she would love to spend her 30 minutes of observation, but procrastinated until the last moment and improvised with a late-night walk, followed by a few minutes of sitting on her balcony. Even though the night walk wasn't what she had planned, she was still amazed by the power of observation. She didn't walk anywhere new; in fact, it was a walk she had taken countless times, and yet she was amazed by how "new" it felt when she truly paid attention to her surroundings. She noticed an art shop tucked right next to the dry cleaners that she had never seen before, and at the corner there was a little free lending library that looked like it hadn't been used in a while. It was almost as though she was a visitor experiencing the neighborhood for the first time.

Similarly, David Kelley, founder of IDEO, recommends thinking like a traveler. When you travel to a new country, you pay attention to every detail, delighting in the new smells, sights, and sounds of your location in a way you don't at home. David suggests that simply being acutely aware of your surroundings will help you spot more opportunities. This leaves us wondering. What opportunities are present in our classrooms that we haven't stopped to notice? What would happen if we questioned all our practices as though we were travelers? What might we notice if we truly stopped and took a few minutes to observe the practices in our schools? Our guess is that not only might we notice opportunities, but we might also begin venturing into new solutions. How might you hone your powers of observation?

Challenge yourself to find something new in the mundane. Do you always spend time in the school office? What are you missing? Instead of sitting in your office, sit in the chairs usually reserved for those waiting to meet with you. Settle in and observe. What new details emerge? Look around slowly. Does this perspective give you new insights into what a student, parent, or teacher must feel when they sit on this side of your desk? Just because you have looked at something a hundred times doesn't mean you have seen it. Joan, a principal of a K–6 school who had been in the position for many years, decided to observe, from a different perspective, something she had been part of year after year. It was the day class lists and teacher assignments were posted in front of the school, the week before school started. This was a favorite day for Joan, since she loved welcoming back the students and families and was always filled with possibilities for the new year. Unlike many colleagues, Joan chose to be present, chatting with families, even if it meant having a few uncomfortable conversations with parents or students who weren't pleased with their class assignments. This year, though, Joan decided to just observe. She parked her car across the street and watched. Sure, there was some excitement and happiness to be observed, but she also saw a different side to the day. She noticed the kids who feigned excitement in front of their friends while looking at the list, but then walked away with their heads down, fighting back tears. She noticed parents getting on their cell phones, having agitated conversations as they left school. Maybe the day wasn't as great as she had perceived it to be. Could there be a better way? The simple act of observing and really seeing something she had been a part of left Joan questioning and imagining different solutions. Joan was so intrigued by what she observed, she followed up with parents to dig deeper and really understand both their and their children's experiences. What might you try to really see for the first time?

Immersion Insights: Shadow a Student (or a Teacher)

Consider shadowing a student or a teacher for an entire day and putting yourself in their shoes: walk the halls they walk, sit in their seats. What is their daily experience at school? The aha moments that you will get from this experience are worth the time out of the office. They are rich, human-centered, and powerful. In fact, administrators and teachers who have tried this often credit it as the number-one thing that helped them shift their role from accidental designer to intentional designer. What might happen if you viewed your role and approach as a principal through the eyes of your students? Or through the eyes of your teachers? How might that shift your focus?

The first time Alyssa intentionally shadowed a student was on the first day of a new school year. She thought it would be interesting to view the "back-to-school" excitement through the student's eyes. As a student, she had participated in plenty of first days, and yet, she was in no way prepared for the reality or the boredom of what she experienced. She was shadowing an 8th grade student in a traditional middle school setting with a seven-period day. The welcome-back excitement from the students arriving at school carried into the first-period class, when there was a quick "get-to-know-you" activity followed by a review of the rules, syllabus, and expectations. It was very teacher-centric, with little effort to engage or encourage participation from the students. The class went by fairly quickly, but then she realized she would likely be repeating this same class structure six more times in different content areas. By period four, she was bored beyond belief. She found it hard to muster enthusiasm in any of the classes. With the newfound knowledge from her experience, she brought a novel idea to the leadership team: redesigning the first three days of school. The team brainstormed ways to make the first three days more about building a learning culture and cultivating relationships among and between students and teachers. What a perfect opportunity for a redesigned experience, one that, unless looked at through the eyes of a student, may not have been apparent.

Erik Burmeister, former principal of Hillview Middle School in Northern California, took shadowing a student a step further by creating a small "design team." The design team identified a problem: how might we use time and resources differently to better meet the needs of our students? The team knew the best place to start was with students. They identified profiles of different types of students attending their school and assigned each member of the design team to a specific student. Design team members shadowed a student for an entire day, following up with an interview of the students and their parents. This perspective of new data helped them approach the allocation of resources from the perspective of what was best for students. The outcomes included a new bell schedule, master schedule, and intersessions that look almost nothing like a traditional middle school. Now design and empathy are so second nature that they are both just business as usual at the school.

Because we are often short on time, it can be tempting to only shadow for one period or a small portion of the day. While you can learn some things from a short experience, it doesn't paint the entire picture. The more time you can give to the shadowing experience, the deeper your understanding will be, and you will walk away with a clearer picture of possible needs. It can also be tempting to select an "average" student to shadow, one who is having an okay experience at school. We challenge you to think about your "extreme users" when selecting a student to shadow. How is school working for second-language learners? What about exceptionally gifted students? By selecting students who might have needs outside the norm, you will likely gain additional insights.

Another piece to consider is the messaging to those around you and the person you are shadowing. Taking the time to explain your purpose will put those you are hoping to observe in their natural environments at ease. If people are unsure why you're following them around, they may become uncomfortable, and you will not have a genuine view of what they are experiencing. Finally, think through how you will record your observations. Where will you position yourself? What type of notes will you take? How can you be that "fly on the wall" with little disruption to those around you?

Shadowing a student has become so popular that School Retool, an IDEO professional development fellowship that helps school leaders redesign their school culture, actually sponsored a "Shadow a Student Challenge" last school year. During the first challenge, they had over 1,300 principals clear their calendars for the day and spend it immersed in the school lives of their students.

Active Listening

Another way to build empathy for those in your school community is just to listen—really listen—to people. Listen with your ears, eyes, and heart. We are amazed at the number of times people check their phones mid-sentence during a conversation. We get it; we are all connected and must be reachable at any given moment of the day, but we challenge you to start really listening, with all electronics out of sight. Be in tune with the person you are talking to, in tune with their facial expressions and body language. It sounds so basic, but the things we say account for only 7 percent of the total message that other people receive. The other 93 percent of the message that we communicate when we speak is in our tone of voice and body language (Businessballs, n.d.). Pay attention to the other person and try to remove your ego from the equation. Anything you learn is not really about you or how you like things to be done; it is all about what is best for students. When you are ready to take your active listening to the next level, try interviewing for empathy.

Interviewing for Empathy

Borrowing from ethnographic methods, interviewing for empathy is an important step in the design process. The goal of empathy interviews is to have conversations with end users (students, teachers, and parents) that are fairly open-ended and allow you to identify their needs, both explicit and implicit. They are one of the best methods for gathering information and, unfortunately, are not commonly used in schools. Many schools are open to gathering feedback, but they usually do so through surveys. Surveys can help you quickly gather information from large groups of people, but they usually lead to surface-level insights and lack real depth of understanding why a group of people answered a question in a particular way.

In contrast, empathy interviews are designed to gather deep information about fewer people's experiences. In empathy interviews, the interviewer works to build rapport and then evokes stories from the interviewee, really trying to understand his or her point of view and perspective. Interviewing for empathy requires you to ask, "Why?" a lot. Even if you think you know the answers, when you try asking people why they do or say the things they do, sometimes the answers will surprise you. Unlike other interviews, empathy interviews don't require a lot of questions. A conversation that stems from one question should go on as long as it needs to. Because we are trying to understand specific examples, try to stay away from "usually" or "always" when asking questions. Instead, ask about a specific instance or occurrence, such as, "Tell me about the last time you _____." Our perception of reality is often slightly different than our actual reality. For example, many people will state that they are fairly health-conscious, and if you ask them what they usually eat for dinner, they might give an example of grilled chicken and veggies. However, if you asked what they ate for dinner the previous night, their response might be pizza, as they were coming home late from baseball, and the night before was hamburgers, because they were running to another event. You get the point: our "usually" and our reality are often quite different.

Empathy interviews encourage stories. Whether or not the stories people tell are true, stories reveal how people think about the world and their perceptions about the topics you are discussing. Also, watch for inconsistencies between what people say and what they do; these inconsistencies can offer a lot of interesting insights. We talked to a principal at one school who told us that they truly valued student input, and then we watched him not ask one question while we toured classrooms. This led to an interesting conversation around the meaning of student input. And lastly, don't be afraid of silence. Sometimes it takes a minute for people to warm up or to recall a story of interest. Figure 2.1 shows a guide for an empathy interview we used to learn more about the students' homework experience at a school. It is important to note that these interviews are not like job interviews; you don't have to ask every person the same set of questions. Because the goal is to evoke stories, think of the questions as a set of guidelines, rather than a script to be strictly followed. If an interviewee has something interesting and juicy to share, you might only need to ask one or two questions during the interview.

Figure 2.1

Sample Empathy Interview Script: Student Interview on Homework

- Tell me about last night's homework.
- What was your worst homework experience this year? Why was it your worst experience?
- Tell me about a time when homework really helped you. What did that look like?
- Do you ever get stuck doing your homework? Tell me about it.

General prompts to use if you get stuck:

- Why? Why did you do/say/think that?
- Really? And why was that? What do you think would help with that?
- Can you say more about that? Tell me more.
- What were you feeling then? Why?

The good thing about empathy interviews is you can do them virtually anywhere and they don't cost anything. Empathy interviews can be informal or formal, random or scheduled, topic-focused or open-ended. Because you are focused on learning about someone's experience, you can learn a ton, regardless of how you choose to structure them. When Alyssa was an administrator, a conversation she had with a middle school student during lunch helped her see what it was like for students to receive their report cards in the mail and caused her to rethink how we shared feedback with students. She asked herself questions like, "Is a grade on a report card sufficient information for a student?" and "Shouldn't receiving something in the mail from school be a positive experience?" On a grander scale, empathy interviews conducted over the course of six months with numerous students, teachers, and parents helped inform how to improve learning experiences across an entire school district, with the insights feeding into a strategic plan. Regardless of the scale, empathy interviews ground us in the day-to-day experiences of learning and teaching at school.

All you need to conduct an empathy interview is a partner, something to capture your notes, and a handy cheat sheet with suggestions and possible prompts to get you started (see "Tips for Empathy Interviews" in the Appendix). We encourage you to have a partner, when possible, to help document the interview. It can be tricky to be responsible for both interviewing and documentation. During the interview, try your best to capture what you see, what you hear, and what your interviewee might be feeling. Document exact phrases and quotes from the interviews; a lot can be lost in the transcription.

Empathy interviews sound simple, but they are very powerful. The simple act of talking to the user moves the conversation from abstract discussions to real interactions. We no longer have to guess or assume what parents are experiencing; we can ground our efforts to improve parent collaboration in the stories and experiences we gather from real parents at our school. We don't have to guess if the supports we are offering for new teachers are meeting their needs; a few interviews with first- and second-year teachers will provide us with actual information.

In 2016, Kyle Schwartz, a 3rd grade teacher at Doull Elementary School in Denver, Colorado, authored a book titled *I Wish My Teacher Knew: How One Question Can Change Everything for Our Kids*. The book describes Kyle's experience of wanting to get to know her students better and asking all students to finish the sentence "I wish my teacher knew . . . ." What her students shared was both heartbreaking and insightful. Student responses included the following: "I wish my teacher knew that my dad works two jobs and I don't see him much." "I wish my teacher knew that my family lives in a shelter." "I wish my teacher know [sic] that I am smarter than she thinks I am" (De La Cruz, 2016). That simple prompt profoundly changed how she approached students in her classroom. What do your teachers wish you knew about them? Engage in empathy interviews. You will likely uncover interesting insights, but if nothing else, getting away from your desk and out of meetings to spend time with the people whose lives are impacted by what your school does can be incredibly informative and rewarding.

Sí, Se Puede: Empathy Interviews Lead to Insights

Under the guidance of Donna Teuber, Richland School District Two (RSD2) in Columbia, South Carolina, runs an R2 innovation incubator and hub. R2 Innovates provides a safe space, mentoring, and support for a team of educators and leaders who want to implement promising practices in their schools and beyond. While R2 Innovates boasts many success stories, *Sí, Se Puede* may just be at the top of the list. This team of five educators from across the district connected around a common interest: solving the learning challenges of a growing Latino population, many of whom speak English as a second language (Sí, Se Puede means "Yes, We Can" in Spanish). This team sensed a lack of connection between school and home for students, but didn't just act on their assumptions. The team chose to verify and make sure that they really understood the problem, which meant talking to and learning from the right people. They questioned how to best reach Latino parents. Their first attempt was an e-mail survey, and they immediately recognized how skewed the results were. What about the parents who wouldn't or couldn't complete an e-mail survey? So the team had to get creative, push further, and figure out how to speak to the right people to get to the core of the problem. They needed to spend time in the community. They went door to door, talking to parents of some of the most disadvantaged students. They went three or four times in the first month, scheduling visits on either weekday nights or weekend mornings, when they were most likely to catch working parents at home. The team also held focus groups in the neighborhood and at school sites. Upon reflection, the team learned the most from empathy interviews. Among their insights were the following:

- Sometimes the students, especially in middle school or high school, may have become proficient enough with English to navigate the system, but that doesn't mean their parents have.
- Families missed the celebrations from their home culture, and as a result, school just fell flat here for them. Parents reminisced about the parties they had in Mexico at the end of every school year. Parents were looking for more recognition, festivities, and opportunities to connect on a personal level at school.

These insights led directly to changes in programs for students. *Sí, Se Puede* created *Fiesta Conexiones*, a summer festival supporting Spanish-speaking students and their families in connecting with school, district, local, state, and national resources. They also created a student interpreter program that provides internships for upperclassmen at Spring Valley and Richland Northeast High to build skills in interpretation and translation, and support Spanish-speaking students and families. Students are able to earn a "Translator Certificate" and course credit, and if desired, can receive assistance in obtaining a business license so they can offer freelance translation services outside of school. *Sí, Se Puede* has also been instrumental in implementing student-led conferences across the district and providing Internet access in homes where needed, and is now working on a college cohort pipeline focused on developing relationships between RSD2 and local universities to encourage Latino students to continue their studies after high school. This team not only had incredible passion to solve their problem, but they also understood the importance of employing empathy prior to developing solutions. *Sí, Se*

Puede is now in its third year and going back out to do another round of empathy interviews before determining its next steps.

Reverse the Interview

When teaching others about empathy, you can even reverse the empathy interview, giving others the opportunity to interview and practice their empathy skills on you. Suzanna Jembsy, head of the Galloway School in Atlanta, Georgia, saw an opportunity to do just that. When first joining the school, Suzanna didn't have a need for a large office and opted for a smaller space. It was in need of decorating, so she turned the task over to a group of students. The students interviewed their new head of school about her work preferences, likes, and needs. They listened well and created a spectacular space that brings joy to Suzanna every time she works in her office. Is there a topic students or faculty could interview you about? Providing the opportunity for the interview and the ability to act on any insights just might be the jump-start that your students or faculty need.

Empathy Mapping

Observation and interviews can give leaders a surprising amount of information. Empathy mapping can be a great way to synthesize your learning and insights around specific users, helping you hone in on their specific needs. There are many different versions of empathy maps available, but most have four common quadrants: thinking, seeing, doing, and feeling. Figure 2.2 includes the four quadrants, as well as two additional sections—pain and gain. The next part of the process takes a bit of role-playing. Imagine that you are one of your students, teachers, or parents. Use the information gathered through observations and interviews to identify what they are thinking, seeing, doing, and feeling. Get specific. Fill the empathy map with sticky notes for each of the four quadrants. If you can, venture into the pain and gain sections of the empathy map. The pains will include their fears, frustrations, and the obstacles they need to overcome. This section will uncover possible causes for why your end users may not be reaching their goals. In the gain section, jot down any insights you have about their success and how they obtained it. What works for them?

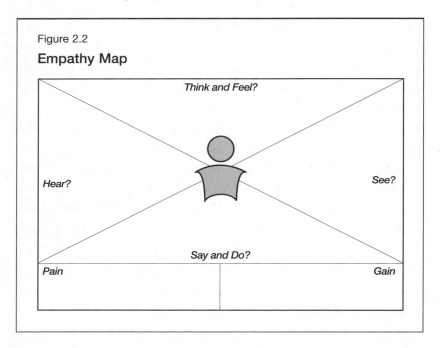

Figure 2.2
Empathy Map

Think and Feel?

Hear?

See?

Say and Do?

Pain

Gain

After creating an empathy map, try to summarize it. Do you have any new ideas about how to approach solutions for your students or teachers? The completion of empathy maps is a great collaborative exercise. If you have engaged in this activity with a team, encourage each member of the team to share their thoughts about the exercise and the end user (student, teacher, parent). Have they identified any new needs? What insights have they gained? With this new information, try creating a needs statement: "Our students (teachers, parents) need a better way to_____BECAUSE_____." This statement is very important, as it will drive your next steps.

We once worked with a school district that was seeking to provide their teachers with higher-quality professional development. From an empathy map we created during a design session, we were better able to identify the needs of teachers. Originally, the focus of our work was to improve teacher professional development, but after interviews with teachers, we completed the empathy map and a very different need emerged. Here is how we summarized the new information: "Teachers need a better way to connect and network with other teachers, both formally and informally, to share best practices, stories of what works, and challenges, because teaching is inherently isolating." Armed with a new needs statement, we were ready to create experiences that met this need. As a result, our next districtwide teacher professional development was conference style, with lots of teacher choice. We added an evening event prior to the professional development day, with a thought-provoking speaker and a happy hour sponsored by local restaurants. Then the actual professional learning day consisted of many sessions teachers could select from to meet their own needs, and we added working lounges and coffee carts so teachers could meet to debrief after a session or plan next steps. None of this would have been created had we not taken the time to empathize with our users via an empathy map.

Be Vulnerable

Empathy is a two-way street. Yes, a very important skill in building empathy is listening, but equally as important is learning to take risks in conversations. This can be hard as a leader, yet removing our masks and revealing our feelings to someone is vital for creating a strong empathic bond. Liz Wiseman, business consultant and author of *The Multiplier Effect: Tapping into the Genius in Our Schools,* talks about the importance of leaders crafting and sharing a "mistake story." A mistake story explains a time when you as the leader made a mistake: what happened, where you went wrong, and what you learned from it. Try crafting a mistake story and think about an opportunity to share it with your teaching staff. By taking a risk and being vulnerable, you will have a double win. Your staff will have more respect for you as a leader, and you will also build your empathy skills.

The first time Alyssa shared a "mistake story" with her staff, she was worried they would judge her mistake as a sign of incompetence. It was spring, and teacher emotions were generally high, as everyone knew there would be staffing changes due to a few enrollment bubbles. One particularly tricky situation was with a 3rd grade team of teachers—three veteran teachers and one first-year teacher. This grade level would only need three teachers the following year and would need to lose a teacher to the 2nd grade team. In working through the decision, Alyssa had multiple individual and group conversations with teachers on the 3rd grade team about what would be best for students. In her eagerness to support and work through the problem with this team, she forgot to have equally important conversations with the 2nd grade team, and rumors started flying. She was baffled that she had forgotten such an important piece to this complicated puzzle. She chose to share her mistake with the staff in full transparency of where they were, what information was being considered, and how the decision would be made. The staff's reaction was deep appreciation and surprising compassion. They understood that everyone makes mistakes. As a new principal, it can be tempting to pretend to have all the answers, but Alyssa found that by sharing her mistakes, others were more willing to share theirs. As a result, they co-created a culture of transparency in which mistakes were learned from and empathy grew.

One thing to remember when sharing a personal mistake story is that most people can sense insincerity. Really put your self-reflection skills to work and think about the story you are telling. Does it ring true? Does it feel honest? Is it significant or trivial? Being vulnerable is risky, so it can be tempting to choose a light story but then embellish or exaggerate the experience. While we don't believe you need to bare your soul in an embarrassing or gut-wrenching way, you do need to carefully think through your story, setting your intention and sincerity for sharing. Another caution: don't take it to the extreme. Successfully sharing a mistake story once doesn't mean you should do it at every meeting. For best results, use this strategy sparingly and avoid the over-sharing syndrome. Vulnerability can be a powerful tool for building trust in your community, but you can easily wear it out or make it feel false with overuse.

Share in Other People's Stories and Experiences

Empathy isn't just about sadness. It really is about listening to and understanding the experiences of the people around you. Some of these stories will be joyful—enjoy them! In early 2017, IDEO's Teachers' Guild launched an empathy campaign called "This Is Me and I Matter." The campaign invites students to share short videos stating who they are and what they want others to know about them. In viewing these videos, teachers will consider the dimensions of stereotyping, reflect on how they see themselves, and create space for dialogue and understanding. The Teachers' Guild launched this campaign because they believe greater empathy can be transformative for classrooms and schools by helping students feel more connected, supported, and safe. What might it look like to launch a #knowmystory campaign at your school?

Working on any of the strategies shared—observing, immersion through shadowing a student (or teacher!), interviewing for empathy, creating an empathy map, and being more vulnerable—will build your empathy skills. Simply viewing the world through a more empathetic lens will raise your awareness of the differences that make your teachers and students unique and prompt you to question the way in which your students or teachers are experiencing your school—a critical first step on your path to becoming a design-inspired leader.

Chapter 3

Opportunity Seeker

Success is where preparation and opportunity meet.

—Bobby Unser, American racecar driver

When Kami first learned about Stitch Fix, she thought, "Who needs this? What a silly concept." Stitch Fix is a service that sends women five new articles of clothing each month based on a fashion profile that they create. A fashion advisor "styles" your personalized picks, adds a note to each box explaining why they chose those particular pieces, and shows you three different ways to incorporate each piece into your wardrobe. You can give input before a shipment if you are looking for a particular item or style, or you can just enjoy the surprise. The investment cost is minimal. You only keep items that work for you and return everything else by dropping it in a mailbox in a prepaid postage bag. Low risk. Kami's friends were all signing up and, although she was a bit hesitant, she wanted to be part of the fun. It was so exciting when the first box arrived! The anticipation of discovery was high, and she opened the box with a mixture of hope and trepidation. Kami loved it. While she didn't keep everything from that first box, she enjoyed the experience and became hooked on a service she didn't know would make her life so much easier. Stitch Fix has become so popular that they have expanded the service to include men's fashion. It will be interesting to see if this meets a need for men in the same way it does for women.

Companies are seeking new opportunities to fill needs that we didn't even realize we had. Often, these new opportunities are hidden in our everyday habits and routines. The next wave of consumerism is focused less on the product and more on the experience. Innovation is often about seeing opportunity in the everyday and being able to clearly identify a need where you didn't know one existed. Where might there be unmet needs in your school or district? As an Opportunity Seeker, you recognize that each unmet need or problem may actually present incredible opportunities.

Problem Finding

Being wrong until you are right. Are there any other options for people who seek to innovate?

—Seth Godin, American author, entrepreneur, marketer, and public speaker

Think of all the decisions that you make in a day. Our guess is that whether you are in a classroom or an office, you multitask during much of your day, making decisions at lightning speed and solving problems without the luxury of really pausing to think. While we may think that we are great at accomplishing many things at once, research has proven that our brains do not function well when we multitask, and our performance suffers.

For most of the day, our brains process quickly, guided by our past knowledge and experiences. We are efficient. We are problem solvers. Most of the time, these well-worn patterns of behavior are our friend, as they help us survive, but these efficient behaviors can also be our greatest downfall. In our quest to move things along expediently, we can be in danger of applying our tried-and-true problem-solving strategies to the wrong problem. Taking time to question the problem we are facing may lead us to a different approach in solving it.

Problem finding is a skill that Opportunity Seekers have mastered. Unfortunately, it is also a skill and process that is undervalued in many educational organizations. With all the changes needed in education, we rush to formulate solutions and check things off our never-ending to-do lists, hurrying to move on to the next item on the list. When a leader faces a problem, it is common practice to offer a solution immediately, asking few questions. In fact, the team that has the problem is likely to be directly asking for "the answer," feeling a sense of relief when the leader offers a well-packaged solution. As the complexity of the problems our schools face increases, it becomes even more important to formulate better questions and to fully understand what we perceive to be the problem. Not clearly identifying our problems can actually hinder our ability to innovate and effect lasting change.

In a study by the Conference Board, a U.S. business group gave 155 public school superintendents and 90 private employers a list of cognitive capacities and asked them to rate these capacities according to which were most important in today's workforce. Superintendents ranked "problem solving" as number one, but the employer executives ranked it number eight, listing "problem identification" as their top-ranked ability (Lichtenberg, Woock, & Wright, 2008). Most school leaders find problem solving to be a highly valuable skill because it's what we practice every day. Problem solving as our primary driver of change has worked for us in the past, but as evidenced in the study, problem solving is no longer enough. How do we know that we are solving the right problem? Problem identification and definition is a crucial skill for leaders. When Steve Jobs set out to build the iPod, he defined the problem as "1,000 songs in my pocket" (itechgear, 2011). We often wonder: what might be possible in education if we were able to identify and define "problems" as well as Steve Jobs?

In one district, a team of kindergarten teachers came together to solve a problem through their district's innovation incubator and hub. Typically, the incubator encourages teachers from across multiple schools to form teams, but in this case, the teachers were all from the same school and were focused on creating flexible learning environments. After listening to the team talk, the designer of the innovation incubator knew the problem went deeper than creating physically changeable classrooms. She pushed the team to reexamine the problem they were trying to solve. Through research and empathy work, the team realized the issue was less about furniture and much more about how they were personalizing learning for students. Had they not been encouraged to spend time in the problem-identification phase, they easily could have spent time solving a problem they didn't have.

Defining the "True Problem"

It's so much easier to suggest solutions when you don't know too much about the problem.

—Malcolm Forbes, American entrepreneur

Almost everyone's first step to problem solving is suggesting solutions. We rarely stop to ask a clarifying question, dig deeper into the issue, or even listen to the entire problem. We jump right to "here's what I think" mode, throwing out ideas and solutions to the problem. And most likely, no matter how well an issue is presented, everyone hears the problem and understands it somewhat differently. This isn't anyone's fault. As a quote ascribed to the Talmud reminds us, "We don't see things the way they are; we see things the way we are." Our different background experiences come into play, our relationships with the participants have an impact, and our own needs influence the solutions that we suggest. Visit an exhibitor hall at any educational conference and you will see solutions to all sorts of problems, likely some you didn't even know you had. In some cases, vendors selling these "solutions" find themselves debating and defending why their solution is so much better than what previously existed, leaving you to question if there ever was a problem to be solved in the first place. Let's try to avoid the vendor trap by spending more time understanding our problems from multiple perspectives.

Reframing Problems as Opportunities

When Alyssa was working as an assistant superintendent of a mid-sized school district, one of the tasks that fell to her department was the scheduling of a team of music and physical education teachers that traveled to seven different elementary schools. As you can imagine, the schedule was complex; not only was travel involved, but students had choice in what instrument class they took, instrumental music class backed up to PE class, and these instructional minutes provided the classroom teachers with contractual prep time. The system had been in place for years, with several known issues. What happens when a student opts out of taking instrumental music? How do you balance the instrumental sections when students get choice? But no one ever seemed ready to tackle the schedule. There was very little wiggle room, and yet Alyssa knew there had to be a better way to optimize the experience, for both the students and the traveling teachers involved. She tried everything. She printed out complex schedules. She drew on whiteboards and moved sticky notes around. She spent so much time with this problem, she was literally dreaming about schedules at night. She felt like there was an obvious solution, and yet she was stuck. It was making her crazy. Alyssa actually had to walk away from the problem and come back to it with a fresh perspective. She revisited the problem and, to help reframe what she was looking at, asked herself the following questions:

- What am I actually trying to solve? Am I solving a symptom of the problem or am I solving the core of the problem?
- What would happen if I didn't solve this problem? Who would be impacted and what would that look like?
- What are the hidden opportunities in this problem?
- What constraints have I self-imposed on this problem?
- What if I'm the problem? Am I too close to the problem? Who might be able to share new insights and fresh perspectives?

By stepping away from the problem and asking these questions, Alyssa was able to see that her self-imposed constraints had prevented her from coming up with solutions. Sure, the program had always been instrumental music and PE, but that didn't mean that was all it had to be. She was able to remove this "artificial constraint," and a whole new world of possibilities opened up. What if they included choice beyond the type of instrument? What if they were able to allow for fine arts choices outside of music, like drama and dance? By removing constraints, they were able to get creative. They developed a new fine arts block for students that expanded their learning opportunities and solved many of their original challenges.

This is the essence of positive reframing: taking what appears to be a difficult situation and finding ways to turn the problem into something positive. The power of reframing is that it forces you to harness your creative thinking to achieve new solutions. When you use positive reframing, you actually view problems differently. Instead of first exploring how to get the problem to go away, challenge yourself to ask, "What is the opportunity here?" If you still feel stuck, step away from the problem and come back to it using the five questions above.

Shifting Perspectives

When you're stuck on a problem and struggling to positively reframe it, try explicitly looking at it from a different perspective. This might be all you need to come up with a great solution. The ability to successfully look at problems from different points of view comes from empathy, which we explored in the previous chapter. You can practice shifting perspectives by finding the humor in the situation, getting outside your bubble, and using a perspective matrix.

Believe it or not, shifting perspectives or reframing can be taught through jokes. In fact, most jokes are funny because they switch perspectives in the middle of a joke. A great exercise to increase perspective-taking is to create captions for humorous pictures. Think this is easy? Try *The New Yorker* online cartoon caption contest; it is one of the more difficult contests to enter. Each week, *The New Yorker* provides a cartoon in need of a caption. Readers submit their captions, three finalists are chosen, and readers vote for their favorite. It is entertaining to go online and see the three finalists and the very different perspectives shared.

Another strategy to increase your ability to shift perspectives is simply to challenge yourself to get out of your "filter bubble," a term that describes a distorted view of the world resulting from uber-personalized experiences. In today's world, it is easier than ever to surround yourself only with people who share similar viewpoints and perspectives. We are able to curate all our news feeds through Facebook, Twitter, and Instagram, so that we might not ever see that there are people with differing points of view. Now, you may say, "I know some people do that, but not me!" The Kind Foundation is challenging that notion with research that indicates only 5 percent of us regularly see posts on social media that we'd say "differ greatly" from our own world-view. Living in filter bubbles certainly does not help us build empathy or shift perspectives. It actually allows us to comfortably exist without ever challenging our own views.

The good news is that, like most things today, there is an app for that. The Pop Your Bubble app scans your Facebook profile for likes, shares, and friends to get a sense of who you are and the type of news you choose to expose yourself to. Then it offers you a challenge by encouraging you to follow people who hold radically different views than you. Getting outside of our own bubbles can make us better, more empathetic people. My guess is you won't agree with everything you'll find in your Pop Your Bubble feed—I know I didn't—but that is the point. It is a good idea to see what other people are saying about the news, politics, or latest hot topics, even if it's just to remind yourself that not everyone thinks the same way you do. Are you up to the challenge? What new opportunities might you find by continually exposing yourself to those who think differently?

Another tool we offer to help you shift perspectives is a simple matrix (Figure 3.1). A perspective matrix helps you identify and look at the problem at hand from a minimum of four perspectives. The perspectives can change, but general categories in schools include students, teachers, parents, and community. Depending on the problem you are trying to solve, you may want to look at different subsets of a population. For example, if you are solving a problem on teacher professional development, your four perspectives might be a brand-new teacher, a veteran teacher, a single-subject teacher, and a multiple-subject teacher. What you are trying to do with the matrix is establish a minimum of four perspectives on an issue and challenge the notion of a problem through each of those perspectives. One of the schools we worked with was struggling with communication, specifically "back-to-school communication." Here are four perspectives on the issue:

Figure 3.1

Perspective Matrix

Perspective 1 _____	Perspective 1 _____
Perspective 2 _____	Perspective 2 _____
Perspective 3 _____	Perspective 3 _____
Perspective 4 _____	Perspective 4 _____
	Problem or Issue	
Perspective 1 _____	Perspective 1 _____
Perspective 2 _____	Perspective 2 _____
Perspective 3 _____	Perspective 3 _____
Perspective 4 _____	Perspective 4 _____

- *New parent:* School starts the second week of August, it's July 30, and I don't have any information. I am feeling anxious and wish I had more information about our new school. Are there meetings to attend? Will I need childcare? Will I need to take off work?
- *Returning parent:* I know we will get information during the first week of August. I remember it came late in the past. I will have to be flexible at work and juggle as best I can when I get the information.
- *School office staff:* We are so busy closing out one school year, we can barely take a breath before we close the office doors the last day of June. After summer vacation, we are ready to start thinking about the new year and will get the information out as soon as possible.
- *Principal:* I tend to work off and on over the summer getting things ready. We have always sent out info the first week of August, and it seems like enough time.

Taking the time to actually identify the different perspectives helped the principal see a real need for new parents. Seeing this so clearly then empowered the principal to make a few changes, and he committed to earlier communication with families. Want to push yourself? Try taking on a perspective of someone you disagree with or who wouldn't solve a problem the way you would.

Invite Others In

When problem solving, it can be easy to go it alone and forget that not only are there other perspectives, but that other people have really good ideas as well. Not everyone will offer their ideas without an invitation. You can structure the invitation to participate depending on the degree of input and involvement you want from others. One of the simplest invitations to problem solving I've seen was done via sticky notes. A principal we once worked with was struggling with a problem and decided to post the challenge on chart paper in the teacher workroom, where people would see it coming and going. Included was an invitation to add their thinking, with a few stacks of sticky notes and pens nearby. Soon, the chart paper was surrounded by thoughts, feelings, and ideas. The longer the challenge was posted, the more ideas were posted. Sometimes people need time to ponder, and seeing a challenge in a visible place can prompt their brain to think deeper. People will move beyond their first "quick-fix" responses to more perceptive and detailed thinking.

Michael, director of professional development at a large public high school, used a similar strategy when he was determined to clean out and rearrange the faculty room. Over the years, the faculty room had become more of a place to store junk and less of a place to eat lunch and socialize. Knowing that solving the faculty lunchroom dilemma was a small but important piece to building a stronger school culture, Michael met the challenge head on. He started by putting up signs on objects in the room: "Do you use this?" "Does this need to be here?" Inviting people to weigh in on smaller decisions along the way helped him clear the room in no time. Prior to Michael tackling the problem, it had been talked about, but no one did anything about it. Michael invited the faculty to be part of the solution, and within months they had redesigned the space and were being intentional about getting everyone together more frequently in the new and improved faculty room. How might you choose to invite people to solve problems with you?

Opportunity Knocks

If opportunity doesn't knock, build a door.

—Milton Berle, American comedian and actor

Opportunity doesn't just happen; we need to actively seek it out. It's a little like becoming a lottery winner. The lottery happens every week, and we all dream about what we would do if we won, but unless we drive ourselves to a place where we can purchase a ticket and then place our money on the counter, the opportunity is not even a possibility. We solve problems every day. They don't all need deep thinking and close examination; however, there may be some winning lottery numbers hidden among them that we may miss if we don't seek them out.

Find and Capture New Opportunities

If you've read a Harry Potter book or seen any of the Harry Potter movies, you're familiar with the game of Quidditch. Quidditch is a magical competitive sport involving flying contestants. Harry plays Quidditch as a seeker, which means he must fly quickly between all of the players, looking for a small object, the Golden Snitch, which is also flying and changing directions. The seeker must be able to see not only the opportunities that currently exist, but must fly into the space of future opportunities, paying attention to a continually changing path if he ever wants to catch the Snitch. The details and strategies of the game are many, and the player's focus must always be changing as he adjusts course, avoids crashing into other players, and works for the win by successfully navigating a new opportunity.

The game of Quidditch, like daily life in schools, is fast-paced, complex, and at times competitive. It can be tempting to wait until the game is over, school has let out for the summer, or things have slowed down to find and chase new opportunities. But unfortunately, opportunities don't always present themselves in that manner. Many times, opportunities are like the fast-paced Snitch, something we have to chase while navigating other obstacles. You must remain flexible and adaptable. Catching the Snitch is about being ready to move when you see the moment.

This can be challenging for schools. We sometimes miss opportunities because we are so busy with the day-to-day work. Opportunity Seekers, like Ashley Auspelmeyer, lead teacher at Studio D, recognize the need to capture opportunities even if they might be a little ahead of current needs. While attending SXSWedu (the SXS EDU Conference and Festival cultivates and empowers a community of engaged stake-holders to advance teaching and learning; https://www. sxswedu.com/), Ashley was drawn to Real World Scholars, an organization that helps bring entrepreneurship to high schools. Currently the authenticity of learning is still a challenge in Studio D. For instance, having students teach their peers about human rights is a good first step, but they aren't yet solving a problem related to human rights. The more authentic the learning, the more likely students are to solve a real problem. Knowing that a future next step was for the staff to bring more authenticity to their learning, Ashley started investigating Real World Scholars and now has a new opportunity for her teachers, with funding when they are ready to jump over that hurdle. Ashley remarked: "I wasn't entirely sure how it would fit, but I am learning to be comfortable with ambiguity while exploring new possibilities and opportunities." What opportunities are flying by you that you could capture?

Find Opportunities in Your Rearview Mirror

Sometimes we are so busy looking forward to new solutions and opportunities that we forget to take the time to look back at what has already been done. We need to actually stop doing and make room for deep questioning and thinking: reflecting. How can we consciously rethink or challenge the way we have always done things without first looking back so as to look forward? Most problems are not new, and we have encountered them in some form or other at an earlier time. Looking at a problem's history can lend an interesting frame. When we do look back, it's usually with a quick glance. A typical response to new ideas we hear when working with schools is, "We tried that and it didn't work." Oftentimes, if we follow up with, "Why didn't it work?" people aren't really clear. They likely never took the time to dig into what went wrong and understand the specifics of the failed solution. Here are a couple of effective ways we have found to look backward.

Five whys. The next time you hear the phrase, "We tried that and it didn't work," ask why, but don't just ask it once. Ask it five times. Don't be surprised if the first response is both simple and defensive; it's natural. Digging deeper and gathering knowledge around the entire experience will tell you more about the process used to implement the solution that failed and help you see the path that led to the failure. When we were working with a junior high school on reallocating time and resources, a possible solution that kept bubbling to the surface was block scheduling, a practice of lengthening the instructional time for classes and holding them every other day versus every day. Any time there was any mention of block scheduling, body language changed, and there was a distinct shift in the group. Sensing some discomfort, we asked if someone could share the history of block scheduling at their school. As expected, we were given a curt response of, "We tried it and it just didn't work here." The five-whys conversation went as follows.

- *Why?* "Block scheduling doesn't work for all subjects."
- *Why?* "Some subjects, like foreign language and PE, are better taught in shorter blocks."
- *Why?* "Our lessons and materials are created for 50-minute classes, not 90-minute classes."
- *Why?* Long pause . . . "Because that is the way we have always done things."
- *Why?* "Because a long time ago someone arbitrarily made the decision that students should attend every subject daily, and the day was broken into equivalent pieces."

Now we have a real conversation. By asking "five whys," we have unearthed a false constraint around why things are scheduled the way they are, and we can wonder together if this is the best way for students to learn.

History mapping. Gather your team and map the recent history of your organization. If you're a teacher, map your last three years of classroom practice. It's helpful to have a range of perspectives for this exercise so you get a consensus of truth. Institutional memory can get in the way of seeing a true pattern to the past, so having a range of input is important. Get gritty here. History contains both positive and negative moments, highs and lows. Map all of it. Looking at your past practices can give you amazing insights into how you've identified and solved old problems and give you a better vision of where you want to go moving forward. When we worked with one elementary school on history mapping, they were able to realize that they had been working on similar problems a couple of times in their recent history, without actually solving the problem. In 2014, the faculty began questioning the effectiveness of their character-building program for students. In 2015, adding conflict managers on the playground and revamping student leadership opportunities were topics of discussion. Then, in 2016, the school had an increase in the number of bullying concerns being reported. The school faculty was expertly navigating each of these challenges, but it wasn't until they mapped them that they were able to see the problems holistically. Taking the time to map their history gave them a new perspective and a different focus on their work that helped shape their future direction.

Divergent Thinking: Moving Beyond the Obvious

Once you have a clearer understanding of your problem, it's time to get creative in your problem solving. This is where things start to get really fun! In order to move beyond the obvious solution and into more innovative ideas, you need to practice building your creative confidence and divergent thinking skills. Divergent thinking is more than thinking outside the box; it's thinking without the box and figuring out how to create the structure later. Divergent thinking is broader than brainstorming. Brainstorming is one of the better-known techniques that encourages divergent thinking, but there are other techniques. People are sometimes uncomfortable with divergent thinking because it really does push them beyond their comfort zones. It takes practice and a culture that's accepting of risk, since you're asking people to think beyond the first response.

What If . . .

Those two little words are quite possibly our favorite two words when combined, because together they have so much power. The utterance of these two words opens up a world of possibilities and signifies that the person asking them doesn't have all the answers and is open to exploring new ideas. One person asking, "What if . . . ?" is intriguing; a collective group of thought leaders or educators within an organization asking, "What if . . . ?" is powerful.

When working in Los Altos, California, we structured a "What if . . . ?" conversation with a group of 20 administrators, teachers, parents, and school members, all focused on brainstorming ideas that could improve learning for students. We structured our "What if . . . ?" conversation to fall in line with our strategic planning process, where we celebrated accomplishments toward our five-year goals and set short-term objectives. So while the process of strategically planning for the future wasn't a new concept in this district, the process of exploring and playing with the unknown possibilities was entirely new. We spent 90 minutes fully immersed in a conversation that was both exhilarating and exhausting! In less than an hour, we brainstormed over 200 ideas that we believed would improve student learning for all students and then narrowed our focus to 50 ideas we felt warranted further investigation and exploration.

Looking back on this work, it is easy to see how much of the district work tracks back to this conversation. The district team went on to create a flexible professional learning space for teachers, created support for teachers in rethinking instruction, hired instructional coaches, and increased professional learning opportunities. Upon reflection, we wonder if any of this would have happened if we weren't actively engaged in "What if . . . ?" conversations.

Brainstorming

When Kami was teaching in the classroom, she would ask students to brainstorm as part of a project and was surprised by how difficult this was for students. They often got stuck. Brainstorming fell flat, and she was disappointed with the results. It was only after learning about Design Thinking and truly digging into the brainstorming process that she realized where she was going wrong as the teacher. She had made the assumption that because brainstorming was so common, everyone knew how to do it. Wrong. Brainstorming is a skill and, as with all skills, it can be taught and learned.

We have all undoubtedly experienced terrible brainstorming sessions. Our negative experiences have typically gone something like this: you run into a meeting, sit down already feeling a little overwhelmed, and the person at the front of the room throws out a topic. They want your best thinking as the group brainstorms ideas. The meeting leader is wildly charting ideas as people shout them out, and your mind is blank. You literally have nothing. After experiencing this, we now realize that our blankness wasn't entirely our fault; the real ownership of an effective brainstorming session lies with the facilitator. It is amazing that anything of value is produced in these types of brainstorming sessions, and usually, just as a few good ideas are emerging, the session is cut short before anyone gets to unpack them and do the really hard, truly creative work. So how do you avoid the terrible brainstorm meeting trap? Try these brainstorming tips to get the most out of the process.

- *Ensure every participant understands their role.* While the perspective of every participant is valued, it is important to clarify roles and set accurate expectations. Participants need to understand that being in the brainstorming session may not necessarily mean that they are making the decisions.
- *Establish and review the brainstorming rules:*
  —Reiterate that there are no bad ideas.
  —Do not evaluate ideas as they come, but
     include everything.
  —Encourage wild and crazy ideas.
  —Defer judgment and push beyond obvious solutions.
- *Give everyone a pen and pad of sticky notes.* The one who holds the pen controls the flow of information in a meeting. During a brainstorming session, we don't want to limit the flow, so give everyone a pen and a pad of sticky notes. As people jot down ideas, have them verbally share and post on large chart paper.
- *Get the group warmed up prior to brainstorming.* Don't expect people to brainstorm cold; give them an activity to warm them up. Try a combine-and-connect activity called

"Two Buckets." One bucket has a list of name brands; the other bucket has a list of product categories. Participants select cards and pair up. Their challenge? Create a new product with the information they were given and design a slogan using six words or less. This is a quick activity that requires all participants to loosen up and begin exploring new ideas. A fun example from one of our teams was a "Harley-Davidson Car Seat" with the slogan "Ride Safe in Style." Quick and silly brainstorms, such as, "How many uses can you think of for a paper clip?" can also get people in a more creative thinking space when you're looking to problem solve. Most times, these activities take less than 10 minutes and, when incorporated with intention, can form part of the first steps toward a more dynamic school culture that embraces risk and change.

- *Provide five minutes of individual brainstorming time.* Even once people are warmed up, it is nice to provide a few minutes of individual brainstorming time. Throw out your topic and give people five uninterrupted minutes to get their juices flowing. This also helps build creative confidence, as people now have ideas to contribute easily once the group brainstorming session begins.
- *Ask for people's worst possible ideas.* Get them out there. Once everyone has shared their worst possible solution to the problem, everything is uphill from there. As an added bonus, sharing your worst idea tends to loosen people up and adds an element of humor to the process.
- *Encourage flair.* Prepare questions that can be used to spur new ideas. The questions are essential, because the way you ask the question will frame all the solutions. Here are a few samples to get you started:

  —What if we could create a school guided by the best instructional, innovative, and creative practices available? What would that look like?

—If money were no object, what instructional practices would we want to see implemented across the grades/school sites?

—If we had the opportunity to visit a school in the year 2113, what would it look like?

—If we wanted to prepare a student to be the individual who cures cancer/solves world hunger/eliminates global warming, what skills would they need to learn and what would their educational program look like?

—What kind of educational program would students create for themselves if given the chance? How could we build in student choice throughout the instructional day?

If these prompts aren't working or you need to get people unstuck, try some more general prompts, such as:

—How would Walt Disney solve your problem? What would Kim Kardashian suggest?

—How would we solve our problem if our school were on the space station or on a new planet?

—What if we removed all technology? What if we were designing for a virtual reality school?

- *Spend time narrowing the focus to provide closure.* After brainstorming in small groups, ask every participant to place a red circle next to an idea with the biggest impact; a blue circle next to a "pie in the sky" idea; a yellow circle next to a quickly implemented idea; and a green circle next to ideas that are the most cost-effective. This narrowing process allows every participant to have a say in highlighting their favorite idea.

Find Your Big Three

Another way to get beyond the obvious is to question your questions. It is helpful to identify your big questions—not those easily answered, but those that make you stop and think for a moment before diving in. Sometimes we are not sure that we started with the right question, and we get stuck. New questions can help us get unstuck.

Identify three major changes that you and your school may be struggling with, and ask three new questions about each of these changes. It is not uncommon for principals to be bogged down with too many initiatives that are competing for their time. Prioritize. Sometimes initiatives get stuck because we are having the wrong conversations. A well-crafted question is one of the best tools to help uncover hidden opportunities. Figure 3.2 presents two initiatives our administrative team was once struggling with and the questions we used to help reframe the conversation.

Premortem

Kami's mother is a worrier. Any time Kami suggests trying something new or different, her mom explains all the reasons why it won't work and may be doomed for failure. Kami has learned to "premortem" new experiences with her. Whenever she has something challenging facing her, Kami walks her mom through all the things that might possibly go wrong, and together they think of all the possible responses for dealing with each of them. While they can't predict every outcome, her mom has a solid plan for different versions of failure, which lowers her anxiety.

At work, we usually end a project with a debrief of what happened; we do a postmortem of the project or event to look at what we could do differently next time. What if we also did a premortem? What if we started by naming risks or elephants in the room, allowing others to voice their concerns and fears? "What could go wrong?" "If this ends in disaster, what would be the consequence?" We could then talk through possible strategies for dealing with failures, and everyone would feel like they had the beginnings of a contingency plan. There will always be unknowns and things that we can't predict, but using a premortem strategy

Figure 3.2

Questions to Get Unstuck

Initiative	Where We Got Stuck	Three New Questions
Rethinking Report Cards	Disagreements about what should be on the report card document, balance of academic indicators/nonacademic indicators, and frequency of report cards.	• What would it take for this to be the last year of students receiving report cards while still receiving quality feedback? • What can we learn from Wells Fargo? (I wouldn't be impressed if the bank told me they were redesigning my bank statement!) • Who needs what type of information? When? For what purpose?
1-to-1 Initiative	Funding the initial devices is one thing, but securing funding for refreshment plans left us unsure of the right direction.	• What if we allowed students to bring devices from home? • What if we were device-agnostic and deviated from being an Apple-only environment? • What if we only provided devices to those students who needed them?

will help you feel more prepared for the unpredictable and may help you push further into risky opportunities.

Get Feedback Early and Often

As you work to find new opportunities, continuous feedback is essential food for the process. Creativity is fueled by the uplifting words and actions of others. Even in the brainstorming process, using the phrase "yes, and . . . " is a feedback tool that promotes a positive dialogue, as opposed to "yes, but . . . ," which shuts down the conversation. Learning to give and receive valuable and meaningful feedback throughout a decision process helps create transparency and invests everyone in the end result. Evaluate your feedback processes.

- Assess how you currently obtain feedback. What processes are in place? How often do you ask?
- What do you do with the feedback you receive? Does it change what you do?
- What opportunities do you currently have to offer feedback to other people or departments?
- Do you actively seek feedback from a least likely source or someone you know will challenge your ideas? Don't be afraid to ask other people to help you get better.

As an Opportunity Seeker, you are passionate and aware of possibilities, unmet needs, and the power of imagination. Problems with great complexity require great creativity. Opportunity Seekers encourage creativity to keep from flatlining in your solutions and reverting to what you know. You see potential where others see problems. When others get stuck by roadblocks, you soar above and are able to see the big picture. You know that progress will happen if you continually forge ahead. Practice sharpening your vision, creating new frames, and moving beyond the obvious solutions, and put your opportunity seeking skills to work.

Chapter 4

Experience Architect

*A mind that is stretched by a new experience can never
go back to its original dimensions.*

—Oliver Wendell Holmes Jr., former Associate Justice of
the U.S. Supreme Court

Always one to get sucked into the latest fitness craze, Alyssa recently ventured into SoulCycle—an indoor cycling class that incorporates both dance moves and arm weights while on a bicycle. These classes are actually marketed as a dance party on a bike. She had heard incredible hype about SoulCycle and was now experiencing firsthand why. From the bright, welcoming lobby smelling of grapefruit to the dark cycling room with loud music, freshly cleaned bikes, and white towels draped across the handlebars, it was apparent that every detail is carefully crafted. The friendly instructors (all trained at "Soul University") act as both fitness coaches and motivational speakers, offering positive reinforcement throughout the class. The walls are covered with quotes such as, "We aspire to inspire" and "We inhale intention and exhale expectations." None of this is by accident; it is all carefully designed to create an experience that makes people feel good. People get hooked on SoulCycle's unique combination of positive reinforcement and endorphins so much that they are willing to pay upwards of $40 per class. Alyssa wandered out of a particularly intense class, a little in awe of the previous 45 minutes, and thought a lot about the curation of such an experience. She started thinking about all the opportunities we have in schools to create learning experiences as impressive and meaningful as what she had just had. She wondered what might happen in schools if we were able to create highly curated and beautifully designed experiences for students. For staff? How might that change the learning that takes place?

An Experience Architect is "a person relentlessly focused on creating remarkable experiences, a person who maps out how to turn something ordinary into something distinctive—even delightful—every chance they get" (Kelley, 2005). We believe that being an Experience Architect is one of the key qualities of any successful school leader. Think of all the experiences you design every day for your teams, for your faculty and staff, for parents, and for students. Each of these presents an opportunity to turn something ordinary into something extraordinary. If it suddenly sounds daunting and exhausting that every staff meeting or lesson needs to be a highly curated and beautifully designed experience, well, you are right. That might not be possible—at least at first. But the more you see yourself in this role, the more you will realize that being an Experience Architect is, like many other elements of leadership, simply a set of behaviors and mindsets that you can learn and practice.

In business, experience design is all about measuring the value from the customers' perspective and continually investigating new areas of value for them. In education, we have to begin by more clearly defining our "customers," or end users.

We believe our primary end users are our students. They should always be first and foremost in our minds when designing experiences, with secondary users being parents and possibly even the broader community. As a principal, there is another group of end users that are equally, if not more, important for you to design for: your faculty and staff. They are the direct link to improving student outcomes. As we work through strategies that will increase your Experience Architect abilities, we are going to share specific suggestions for your work as it relates to both your teachers and students.

Building a Culture Through the Lens of an Experience Architect

Reframing the school's leadership roles can't happen in isolation. Everything we explore together will happen in the context of your school with your staff, students, and community, so we would be remiss if we didn't help you set the stage for building a culture for design-inspired leadership. Culture matters. It is not one of those small things to be dealt with after the "real work" is done. Creating the right culture *is* the real work. The first task of an Experience Architect is to prepare an environment where design-inspired leadership can flourish.

Let's start with a quick assessment of your school culture. Everyone who interacts with your school will likely have their own unique set of words to describe it. Are you curious what the most common descriptions include? You can create a baseline for our later work with a few actions.

Ask the Question

What three words would you use to describe your school environment? Ask everyone. Listen and collect responses, resisting the urge to ask for clarification. There will be time to dive into the why later. As a new principal, Kami was curious how the staff would describe their school and found a way to casually work the question into every conversation she had, making note of the responses. At the same time, she was intrigued and perplexed by some of the most common responses that were surfacing: tradition, events, expectations, and community. Were these the types of words she had hoped she would hear? What could she learn from these responses, and how could she use this information to design the best possible learning environment for students? You must be curious now, ready to discover how people describe your environment. There are many ways to capture responses, depending on the time you have to spend. Here are a few options to consider, listed in order from what takes the least amount of time to process to the most amount of time:

- Exit ticket at a staff meeting
- All staff members share three words on Twitter using a specified hashtag
- Online survey (Google Forms or SurveyMonkey both offer great free tools)
- One-on-one conversations

Kami chose a very informal approach since she was new and didn't want to stifle creativity. Regardless of the approach you choose for adults, we encourage you to ask the same question of students in the hallways, in the lunchroom, or on the playground. While students are usually honest, they quickly learn the benefits of telling adults what we want to hear, so don't be afraid to dig deeper.

Ask More Questions

What are you curious about? What do you find yourself wondering about with the new information you have gathered? Generate additional questions and resist the urge to answer them. These may lead to further exploration. If you are unsure where to start, here are a few questions to get you going:

- What aspect of your school could really use some creative thinking?
- What would delight students? Teachers? Parents?
- What are the challenges in your context that don't have easy answers and might require the mindsets of a designer to help you get unstuck?

Asking questions and learning to be an observer is an essential part of Design Thinking. This baseline information will be helpful as we explore new roles and play with "wicked problems" in education throughout the book. Armed with new information about your school, let's dive a bit further into the school culture to explore creativity and risk.

Creativity Versus Compliance

The culture of school is radically at odds with the culture of learning necessary for innovation.

—Tony Wagner, professor, Harvard University

One of the most difficult challenges in education is our posture toward the possible, which is directly tied to the type of culture created. How would you assess the culture of your school or district? Is it a culture of creativity or a culture of compliance? Figure 4.1 highlights major differences between the two cultures. One culture can feel innovative and welcoming; the other can often stifle ideas and create a less agreeable work environment. The way we lead determines whether our culture is creative or merely compliant.

How does leadership at your school promote or discourage creativity? This mindset begins with the leader and then can permeate every level of an organization. An important job of school leadership is to encourage and reward creative thinking and collaboration, while also recognizing both formal and subtle ways those things are discouraged.

Figure 4.1

Culture of Compliance Versus Culture of Creativity

Culture of Compliance	Culture of Creativity
• Risk is not tolerated	• Risk is encouraged as a natural part of the learning process
• Mandates are valued above all	
• Fear is commonplace	• Creative solutions are valued
• Top-down leadership	• Trust is integral to work and learning
• Language implies singular ownership (my class, my students)	• Distributed leadership, where all are empowered to act
• Constraints are roadblocks	• Language implies group ownership (our school, our students)
• Initiatives are implemented with very little feedback	• Constraints are seen as possibilities
	• Initiatives are quickly implemented with small user groups, lots of feedback gathered, with iterations along the way

Peter Drucker, an author and business consultant, said, "Culture eats strategy for breakfast," but we needn't think of it as choosing one over the other. Using design-inspired leadership strategies can enhance the power of both culture and strategy, connecting the two pieces into a cohesive whole. The good news is that no matter where your school culture currently falls, it can be shifted. One of the greatest tools to use in shifting a culture is improvisation, or improv.

Improv helps build a creative culture and boosts everyone's creative confidence. We were introduced to the concept while attending a workshop where our first icebreaker contained the word "improv." We both had nightmare visions of standing in front of a room full of strangers and trying to be funny. It was a paralyzing thought. Fortunately, the facilitator quickly launched into an explanation of the activity, reducing the apparent anxiety level of everyone in the room. We started with a simple game of "Zip, Zap, Zop," an infinite game that only required tuning in to the group and playing at the speed of fun. It turns out that improv practices have very little to do with being funny and more to do with attitude.

Improv is the ability to say, "Yes, and . . . ." It is a tool that allows for creativity beyond the normal. Think of it as a team sport that requires connections to those around you. You must be present and focused on the now to react to what is being said. It encourages careful listening and acceptance of what is being offered, without judgment. Embracing a designer mindset requires a healthy dose of improv. Practicing the following tenets of improv helps everyone on your team build skills for creative problem solving:

- *Suspend judgment.* When you wait to analyze, you stay present in the creative process, saving the evaluation phase for later.
- *Let go of your agenda.* There is nothing to be accomplished. Let yourself get caught up in the experience.
- *Listen in order to receive.* When you listen closely to others, you can find moments where you can agree and support, building on each other's ideas, rather than evaluating and finding the "yes, but . . . " answers.
- *Get out of your head and concentrate on the group. Make everyone on the team look brilliant.* If you focus outward, you remove the focus from yourself, and the work is about what you are creating together.

Try introducing an improv activity as an opener at your next staff meeting. You may get some startled looks or interesting comments, but with repetition, you'll find that infusing that quick and creative element of fun can create a culture that is ready for change. Don't let any first reactions deter you. Trust the process and encourage your staff to take risks! Here are some great first steps:

- At your next meeting, try a simple icebreaker that focuses on "playing at the speed of fun." An infinite game with no winners works best. "Zip, Zap, Zop" is very easy; below are directions on how to play from the DBI Network (http://dbp.theatredance.utexas.edu/node/29), where you may find even more infinite games to play. "Everyone stands in a circle. Tell them you have a bolt of energy in your hands. To start the game, send the bolt out of your hands with a strong forward motion straight to someone else in the circle (using your hands, body, eyes, and voice), saying, "Zip." Be sure you make eye contact with the person you pass it to. They should receive it and pass it immediately to someone else, saying, "Zap." That person passes it on with a "Zop." The game continues, "Zip, Zap, Zop," with the goal being speed and fun. If there is a mistake, encourage everyone to simply continue playing.

- Or try an activity that encourages people to open up to more possibilities with a quick game of "yeah, but . . ." versus "yes, and . . . ." Partner people up and tell them they will have two minutes to plan a party for their boss. Quickly have them designate who will be Partner A and who will be Partner B. Partner A will start by throwing out a party idea, to which Partner B will respond, "Yeah, but . . . " and give a reason why this is a terrible idea. Have them continue this for the full two minutes. Can you imagine any parties being planned that way? I always ask if anyone has planned an incredible party and the answer is a resounding and frustrating "no." Have them try it again, but this time Partner B is responsible for throwing out party ideas, and Partner A will always respond with, "Yes, and . . . ," building onto the idea. It is amazing how creative and fun the parties get when we build on each other's ideas. This is a great way to start building a "Yes, and . . . " culture of possibility.

Improv allows your team to build something that is truly shared. It requires multiple intelligences and allows for multiple points of view. It improves dialogue and builds communication skills. It is one of the best tools in the designer toolbox for building creative muscle and innovative solutions. A little improv can go a long way to improving the culture of your school. Find more improv resources and games at the Improv Encyclopedia online (http://improvencyclopedia.org/games/).

Designing to the Edges

Fit creates opportunity.

—Todd Rose, author, *The End of Average*

In *The End of Average,* author Todd Rose tells a story about fighter pilots and the need for a custom-designed cockpit for fighter jets in the 1950s. The standard dimensions of the 1926-designed cockpit were no longer working due to an airplane design change, and researchers at Wright Air Force Base in Ohio began gathering data to see how the average measurements of a pilot's height, weight, and body length may have changed. After calculating the averages of the 10 physical dimensions that were most relevant, they wondered how many pilots would actually fit this "average" profile. What they discovered? Zero. Not a single one fit within the average range of all 10 dimensions. Todd Rose goes on to explain how the Air Force made a bold statement: "Ban the average, design to the edges."

What might it look like to "ban the average, design to the edges" in education? Almost everything we use in education has been designed for the average student, and many of our workplace procedures have been standardized with the average teacher in mind. Staff meetings have similar agendas. We roll out initiatives through standard professional development practices accompanied by the required binder, and we talk about our average data numbers. The problem is that there is no such thing as an average student or average teacher. Everyone has a unique, or jagged, learning profile. What if, instead of starting with the average profile, we started with these jagged learning profiles? What might happen if we looked at our staff and our school and saw individuality? Without a doubt, there is untapped potential walking around your campus and sitting in your staff room. But how do you tap into it? We believe the solution lies not in designing solutions for the average, but in designing to the edges. Let's explore in a bit more depth what that means.

Find Your (Extreme) Users

As we have already explored together, the first step to any design exercise must start with a greater understanding of those we are designing for. We can usually identify the middle of the bell curve fairly easily. These are our "average" users and the users we spend most of the time designing around. Yet it's the extreme users on either end that we need to focus on if we want to have a greater impact. Extreme users typically have needs that are magnified in some way—which means they have probably also created workaround solutions that are more noteworthy. By meeting the needs of an extreme user, you create solutions that address a much wider population, solving problems that may not have been visible while the spotlight was focused on the "average" user.

The OXO peeler is a perfect example of what can happen when you design for an extreme user. In 1989, Sam Farber had an aha moment when watching his wife, Betsey, struggle with a common vegetable peeler due to arthritis. He set out to solve the problem for Betsey by creating a vegetable peeler with a fatter handle that was more comfortable to use, inadvertently creating kitchen tools that were easier for *everyone* to use (Smart Design, n.d.). Looking at education, our extreme users may be families that choose to homeschool, families that need before- and after-school care, or families that need flexibility due to special circumstances, such as young elite athletes or students needing home hospital support. Who are your extreme users, and what are their unique needs?

Engage Your Extreme Users

Once you have identified your extreme users, try finding ways to engage with them around the problem you are attempting to solve. Let's pretend you have taken on the task of redesigning student lunch procedures. As a part of this design challenge, you might consider the following:

- How long do students wait in line to purchase their lunch?
- How quickly is food served?
- How many students order school lunch?
- What days are busiest?

Your first inclination might be to only talk to the students who order the hot lunch program, when in fact you may learn more from students who have never ordered hot lunch (why not?) or from those who order hot lunch every single day and are first in line (why?). Then, observe and talk to your extreme users, looking for workarounds or behaviors that uncover insights or inspire thinking. Sometimes these extreme users can inspire wild ideas that help you understand what might resonate not just with them, but with your average users as well.

Narrow Your Focus

Often, when we look at our challenges, we engage with a very long list of reasons something may not be working. Start by creating a list of all the different pieces needed to solve the problem. Going back to our lunch example, create a list of all the lunch procedures.

- How is the food organized for students to pick up?
- How many steps do students go through in the process?
- Where is the line physically situated in the room?
- How many points of contact are there between staff and students?
- Where is the greatest pain point?
- Which solution is most important to start with?

Once you have identified your starting point, you can gather information around that specific need from all your users. You have a focus. Your solution may also end up addressing some of the other needs that you've identified. Regardless, you've started a path toward creating a new experience.

Truly understanding and knowing the needs of all your users will help you create and design unique experiences that fit your school and community. Remember the empathy map and needs statement from Chapter 2? Why not create an empathy map for each of your extreme users? What if we could redesign parts of our schools or jobs to fit the individual? Not only might we utilize undiscovered talents, but we would also encourage and value individual excellence.

Eric Juli, principal of Design Lab Early College High School, an inner-city public school in Cleveland, Ohio, has had to create experiences for a group of extreme users, namely students who attend high school but have never once experienced success at school. Recognizing that students needed to experience success-ful learning, Eric designed X-Block, a weekly three-hour block with no regular classes, worksheets, tests, or contrived school assignments. Students are engaged every week with community partners of their choice, doing real work. They are learning by doing. They are using found objects to create art to cover the walls of a fairly drab school building. They are programming drones, cooking healthy food options, and discovering a love of yoga. Students are repairing bicycles and working to improve the neighborhood, but mostly, through these experiences, they are discovering their voices and learning how to be successful. Some students who hated school and never spoke are completely engaged in their X-Block. Other students, who expect school to be about worksheets and tests, are telling their principal that he is "doing school wrong." It is beautiful and scary all at the same time. School has been set up to be about power and control, textbooks, and rote memorization. When teachers experience how much more powerful it is to work side-by-side with students on real work that matters, it's terrifying for everyone involved. According to Eric, X-Block is the best new piece of their school, even if it isn't perfect. They will continue to refine this new experience based on the needs of their most extreme users.

Let's Design (or Redesign) Experiences

Now that you have a better understanding of how to develop empathy for your end users and have even engaged in thinking about your extreme users, let's start exploring what it might look like to design an experience, or, as in the case of many of the examples we will share, redesign an experience that currently exists. In fact, we have found that a great place to start is with your school calendar. What types of events do you have scheduled? Who is the intended audience? What is the purpose of each of the events? Does the event in its current form meet the needs of the users? How do you know? These may seem like really basic questions to begin with, but it isn't always apparent why we continue to do some of the things we do. Creating quality experiences involves making good assumptions and then testing and iterating based on those assumptions.

Take "back-to-school night," for example. It is an event that happens every year at almost every school across the country. It is generally an evening event that is held within the first few weeks of the school year. While there are variations of this event, the most common one has parents attending the school in the evening to spend time getting to know their children's teacher and learn about the specific curriculums. Almost every teacher I know dreads back-to-school night because they feel pressured to share with the parents all the details of the coming year, and almost every parent I know dreads back-to-school night for almost the exact same reason—they have to try to take in all the details for the entire year in a small amount of time, which gets even more complicated if they have more than one child at the school. So, if back-to-school night in its current form isn't meeting the needs of the parents or the teachers, why do we continue the practice? And what if we spent some time asking our end users, in this case the parents, about their expectations and hopes for the evening?

Mary Beth Miller, a 2nd grade teacher at Oak Avenue Elementary in Los Altos, California, did just that. Before planning what would have been her 15th back-to-school night, she spent time talking to parents and uncovered some interesting needs and wants. She discovered parents wanted to

- *Get to know more about the teacher on a personal level.* As one parent stated: "My child spends six hours a day with you. I want to know about you as a person and how my child will benefit from having you as their teacher."
- *Get to know their children's classmates.* Parents want to have a sense of the students in class with their children.
- *Get a glimpse of a day in the life of their child.* No surprise, but parents don't always get a lot of information from their children about school and want to get a better sense of the types of experiences students will have in this particular grade.

Much to her surprise, Mary Beth discovered that parents were less interested in hearing about the Common Core Standards, textbooks, or assessments—all topics that are typically covered at back-to-school night. With this new information, Mary Beth set out to design a back-to-school night experience that actually met the needs of the parents. The first thing she did was craft and send a letter home, explaining to the parents that this would not be their typical back-to-school night, along with all the detailed information for the year, including class calendar, curriculum, field trips, and more. She asked parents to read all the information ahead of time and come prepared to engage with her and the class of parents. That evening, Mary Beth began back-to-school night with a slide show of the students in class. When their student's picture was projected, the parents were to get up and introduce themselves and their child to the class. The teacher then engaged the parents in learning activities that gave them a better sense of who she was as a teacher, exposed them to the types of learning strategies their children were exposed to, and built a learning community of which they were now a part. The buzz was incredible! Parents left back-to-school night engaged and excited about the year of learning ahead for their children.

What events might need redesigning at your school? Here are a few common school events to get you thinking: schedule day or posting of class lists, first day of school, parent-teacher conferences, open house, and promotion or graduation. While we don't recommend you tackle redesigning all these experiences at the same time, each of them presents a unique opportunity to turn something ordinary into a new experience.

Once you have identified the event you want to redesign, here are a few questions to ask about the experience:

- *Who is involved in this experience?* The more specific you can be, the better. In fact, if you can identify some needs and how the users think, you can start to empathize with their needs.
- *Why is this experience taking place?* Why are people taking part in this experience? What are their end goals, and what do they hope to achieve?
- *What are all the options available?* Challenge your own assumptions about the experience you are planning and play with lots of ideas before settling on the ideas you will execute.

- *Where is this experience taking place (or where would it be best for this experience to take place)?* Is it happening at school, in the teachers' lounge, or in a setting outside of school?

Redesigning with Teachers in Mind

Opportunities for redesigning experiences aren't just found on the school calendar; they can be found almost anywhere. Spend a few minutes in the staff room during lunch, and you will likely walk away with lots of new ideas. The two most common themes we hear from teachers that present fantastic opportunities for redesign are staff meetings and professional development. Sadly, many teachers are not happy with either. What if you were able to transform your staff meetings and truly engage your teachers? What if you were able to redesign professional learning opportunities so that teachers sought out these experiences? Following are four quick guidelines that will help you transform any meeting or event you are planning.

Set the Stage

This may seem trivial or an afterthought, but looking at your meeting space and taking the time to "set the stage" can change the experience. Research suggests you only have seven seconds to make a first impression. While this research is focused on introductions to new people, I believe it holds true to meetings, as well. Think about it. Within seconds of walking into a room, you not only get a feeling about the time you'll be spending there, you also know what type of role you will play. Does the room invite you to engage with others, or compel you to sit in the back row with your eyes glued to your smartphone? Take a quick inventory of your meeting space. What does it communicate? Are you happy with the message being sent? If not, what can you do to change the message? Consider playing music to build energy or calm the room. Think about your seating arrangements. How will participants engage with each other? Does the room physically support those activities? Do you need an improv or team-building activity to help transition people into the meeting? What materials are needed for the meeting? Details matter.

Make It Meaningful

Time is precious, and time together with the entire staff should be protected. To create meetings that are the most meaningful, try running through a few of the questions below for each topic, with teachers clearly in mind, before you place it on the meeting agenda.

- Can any of this information be front-loaded via e-mail or another source?
- Is this information relevant for the entire staff? If not, how might you differentiate sections of the meeting based on participant needs?
- Why is this a priority?
- How will this improve learning for students at our school?
- What is the intended outcome?

If indeed the topic or item earns a spot on the meeting agenda, it's time to think about the best way to facilitate interaction about the topic to get to the desired outcome. We've all sat in too many meetings where the principal or superintendent just casually threw out a topic, hoping for a meaningful discussion. Unfortunately, most times you either hear crickets—because no one wants to contribute—or you only hear the loudest voices in the room, with everyone else silenced. To avoid either of these traps, try the ideas shared in *Gamestorming,* a book by Dave Gray, Sunni Brown, and James Macanufo (2010), which includes more than 80 games. These activities can help you improve communication, break down barriers, and inspire creativity, leading to new insights and strategies. The tools are organized by purpose and will add a facilitative boost to meetings and professional learning sessions. Meetings are like any other part of life; you will only get better if you commit to aiming high. Think about ways to get feedback on the meaningfulness of the meetings.

Allow for Choice

Choice matters, in the classroom and in the meeting room. As a school leader focused on the big picture, it can be easy to fall into the trap of thinking everyone needs information on every topic. But do they? Perhaps you need everyone in the room, but are there places where you can give attendees choices? It may be time to check your assumptions around information sharing. Narrowing the number of your end users may help you design to those edges. Picture your most senior staff and conversely picture your newest teacher; my guess is their needs are vastly different, in what they need both from a staff meeting and from professional learning. One school district fully embraced this notion of choice and voice for its leadership team and moved away from the notion that everyone was required to attend every meeting. Two days before any administrative team meeting, an agenda is sent out ahead of time with information on all the topics being covered. It is made clear whether the topics will be informational or require a quick discussion. There is always an optional time toward the beginning of the agenda for those who would like more discussion, and an opportunity for "new learning" at the end of the agenda. Planning for flexibility and choice goes a long way!

Fun Factor

We believe there should be joy in our work at schools, even at meetings. When designing an experience, consider the element of fun. Yes, we know some work is serious business, but even serious businesses, like banking, are looking to incorporate fun into their experiences. We don't know about you, but we don't always think "fun" when we think of banking. Metro Bank in the United Kingdom is challenging that thinking. Their new tagline is "Banking, but Better." They have completely reimagined the banking experience and are now open seven days a week from 8:00 a.m. to 8:00 p.m. All their branches have a Magic Money Machine that counts coins in the lobby. These machines were intended for kids, but no surprise, you'll find adults using them just as much, if not more, than the younger users. How can you add a fun or interesting twist to the work you are doing?

Los Altos School District iLearn

With these guidelines in mind, we overhauled professional development for teachers in the Los Altos School District (LASD) by primarily focusing on creating meaningful experiences and allowing for choice. Traditionally, professional development is driven by new curriculum or new processes and strategies that are being implemented at the district level. It is usually offered to all staff and delivered to everyone in the same way, similar to how teachers teach a standard curriculum lesson from a textbook. We recognized that teachers were all in different places, with varying levels of expertise and needed areas of growth, and yet our approach for professional learning had been one size fits all. As we set out to redesign professional learning, our goal was simple: engage and inspire our teachers as learners. To accomplish this, we knew we would have to work within the constraints of our teacher contract and think outside the traditional box. Given the limited time we could require teachers to attend meetings, we focused on creating a variety of learning experiences that were so engaging, we hoped teachers would opt-in on nonmandatory meeting days.

Needing a space for these sessions, we turned the old district copy room into the "iLearn Studio" for teachers. It was nothing fancy at first, just a room with tables and chairs where teachers from across the district with a common interest or need could come together to learn. We polled teachers about what they wanted to learn and used this information to create different series of classes. The classes were diverse and included topics such as "Gaming in the Classroom," "How to Use Social Media as a Learning Tool," "Project-Based Learning," and "Design Thinking." Teachers flooded to iLearn. They were excited that we had asked, that we had listened, and that we had created it with them in mind. We even had teachers calling from a nearby district, asking if they could attend our optional teacher trainings. While the classes generally ran from 3:00 p.m. to 5:00 p.m., it was not uncommon for teachers to continue learning and collaborating well past 5:00. It became clear that teachers were hungry for well-designed learning experiences that met their specific needs.

You may not be able to change the professional development offerings for your district, but are there opportunities at your school? Inspired by the success of iLearn, we started to see other incredible learning opportunities popping up around the district. One school started an "appy hour": teachers get together once a month to discuss new applications and technology in the classroom. Another school created a "genius bar" during lunch, where teachers take turns sharing new ideas, student work, and strategies in their classrooms. What are the learning needs of your teachers? How might you plan with those needs in mind? And if you aren't yet ready to take on professional development, how can you apply these strategies to your next staff meeting?

With a little more intentional thought and planning, we can easily design professional development as experiences for both learning and emotional engagement. All great experiences engage both the heart and the mind.

Where Best Intentions Can Go Wrong

Remember to mix it up. Once we discover a process that works really well, it becomes our "go-to" strategy, and we can overuse the strategy. Ours happened to involve sticky notes. We were gathering great feedback through the use of chart paper and sticky notes in our professional development and staff meetings. We were hearing from more people, and the loudest person in the room no longer dominated conversations. But we knew we had fallen into the overuse trap when we overheard a teacher walk into the room saying, "Great. Here come the sticky notes again." It was a sign to shelve the sticky notes for a bit and try some other data-gathering tools. We didn't abandon the sticky notes; we simply mixed them up with some new methods, such as online polls and exit tickets, and then thoughtfully brought that process back when and where it made sense.

A second caution would be in offering too many choices for professional development. This is a lesson Kami learned in the classroom. Currently, offering students choice and voice in their work has become a focus and common practice for many teachers. In the era when curriculum ruled, this was a fairly new practice and seemed very cutting-edge. As technology entered the classroom, the world opened up and students had many more options for how they demonstrated their learning. It was exciting to give them many choices and cool tools. What happened? Students had too many options, and those who were still learning basic skills and needed more direction became lost. The same holds true today with adult learning. We need focus, and while our professional development needs differentiation and options, it is important to think through what those choices look like and evaluate them based on the desired outcomes. All the learning needs to be connected to your bigger picture, and those connections should be easily seen. Carefully crafting your professional development while still allowing choice and voice will create a powerful learning experience.

Aligning Your Experience With Your "Why"

One of the most powerful ways to design an experience is to consistently wrap it around your why. In Simon Sinek's (2013) book

Start with Why, he discusses how great leaders inspire others to take action, and how important it is to have clarity around your purpose. People are more likely to move forward when they have a clear picture of where they are headed, as well as a clear understanding of why they are being asked to do something new.

Reflecting on her teaching career, Kami realized that she sat in too many staff meetings where a new edict was handed out that not only created more work for her as a teacher, but also felt disconnected from what she thought was the direction in which they were headed. Kami left these meetings feeling frustrated and overwhelmed, and, judging by the comments she heard from other teachers, she knew she wasn't alone. In contrast, Kami recently observed a staff meeting where the principal began by highlighting some of the great work that was happening to move their vision forward, reminded everyone of how it fit in with their vision, and then introduced a new requirement of teachers. The new protocol required teachers to record and keep track of all students' physical education minutes during each week to meet a state mandate. Instead of starting with the cold, hard facts of the matter, he began with a discussion, asking teachers how physical education fit in with their why. Why did they believe it was important, how did making time for physical education fit in with their vision, and finally, how might they best record and report physical education minutes each week to meet the state requirement? Staff responded positively and quickly came up with a procedure that felt doable for them. They walked out embracing and understanding the need for the new mandate, rather than frustrated and overwhelmed. The experience was positive and inclusive, rather than negative and disruptive.

The difference in teachers who understand the why is that they are inspired by the work because of their clarity and connection to the why. How might you make your why transparent for all and impact your experience?

Signage: Name It and Claim It

Think about small messages that you can add to your meeting spaces and classrooms to remind people of your goals and purpose. While working with LASD, we co-created LASD Learning Principles (see Figure 4.2) that helped teachers understand the elements of modern learning, and then we made the Learning Principles available to everyone in many different formats. We created posters, bookmarks, and e-mail signatures for people to use. If the message is important, take the extra steps to really brand it and create tools.

Figure 4.2

LASD Learning Principles

Connect experiences. Discover links between learning at school and outside the classroom.

Personalize learning. Use each student's abilities and interests to maximize learning.

Nurture a growth mindset. Create opportunities to reflect and grow.

Process an outcome. Value the approach as much as the result.

Empower students. Help students understand their voice has impact.

Leverage technology. Utilize technology as a tool for learning.

Reference and Remind

Clearly communicate your why in multiple ways. We think we express it enough for everyone to remember and understand, but the more simply you state your why and frame what you do within your why, the clearer it becomes. Challenge yourself to weave all work back to the stated why. Weaving in the why can be as simple as starting every e-mail with the why clearly printed at the top, including it on meeting agendas, providing all staff with a clever e-mail signature to use, or hanging large posters in the staff room. The more we surround ourselves with the why, seeing and hearing it in our work, the more likely we are to internalize it.

Model

Designing an experience around your why is great, but walk the talk. Leaders build trust by continually modeling the change they want to see. Don't simply create the experience; be the experience. If you have ever sat in a professional development session where the facilitator essentially tells you all the ways to engage learners without letting you practicing any of the strategies yourself, you know how frustrating talk without action can be. Don't tell teachers how to do something; show them. You absolutely have to model by example. If you want teachers to use improv in the classrooms, show them how it's done in your staff meetings by playing some improv games. If you want teachers to craft a story for their learners, you need to craft one for the teachers. Challenge yourself to do anything you say is important.

Experiences with a Purpose— Step Outside the Building

Another way to approach experience design is to create an event with a very specific purpose in mind. Perhaps you want to get your teachers to think more creatively. You can create an experience with that goal in mind.

When we work with teachers on a new instructional strategy, the most common request is to see it in action. As educators, we know that the best way to engage students in learning is to make it authentic and relevant, and the same thing holds true for adults. We learn by doing. Most of us remember our school field trips. They stick. Why? Because we were outside our normal learning environment and experiencing things that were not part of our normal routines. Familiar environments cause the brain to tune out, to be less alert and less receptive to new input. When we "get out," we have a new context. So we decided to create authentic out-of-the-box learning experiences for our teachers. Think of them as field trips for adults.

We intentionally planned visits and trips that would allow our teachers to see work in action. When teachers were immersed in project-based learning, we arranged a visit to a school known for project-based learning that would allow our teachers to see both their teachers and their students engaged in the process. Through observation, questions, and conversations, teachers returned with a deeper understanding of project-based learning and had a new vision of the possibilities. When teachers became interested in STEAM—Science, Technology, Engineering, Art, and Math—and were struggling to incorporate these ideas into their lesson design, we arranged a field trip to an art museum. Once there, we worked with a topic expert who led our teachers through hands-on activities showcasing an array of different strategies for adding STEAM to their lessons. Teachers with a growing interest in makerspaces visited a local fabrication lab. They learned how to handle laser cutters and 3D printers, gaining a new appreciation for a truly "hands-on" experience. Getting your staff outside your building can give you a very targeted design experience. It is well worth investigating the resources your community has to offer. Do some investigation, load the bus, and take a field trip!

No Recipe Needed

While experience design is not an exact checklist or recipe to be followed, a template is included in the Appendix that may be helpful the first few times you are designing experiences. Like cooking, the more you engage in the practice, the less reliant you are on an exact recipe. Experience design is a way of thinking that, when practiced, will become more natural over time. Just remember, it all begins with empathy. If you can develop a strong sense of your end users and their needs, you will be more likely to design experiences that meet those needs and delight your users. Think about your own experiences. When was the last time you had a truly great learning experience? What was it and why? Which ones do you remember? What made them memorable? How might you tap into those feelings and create those memorable experiences for others?

Most of the experiences you will design or redesign will in some way be a learning experience. We believe there are a few key elements necessary to constitute a great learning experience. Great learning experiences add value to the learner, are effective first (before any bells or whistles are added), and promote further learning. (Learning for the sake of passing a test is a sad outcome, but that is a conversation for another time.) Designing experiences is such a critical part of any learning process; it is not surprising that some schools are starting to think of teachers as "Learning Experience Designers."

Chapter 5

Rule Breaker

Know the rules well, so you can break them effectively.

—The Dalai Lama

MTV, among the most-watched cable channels in the 80s and 90s, didn't invent video or records, but it pulled them together in an entirely new format. CBS, in contrast, owned both a record company and a television network, but followed conventional wisdom and kept its companies separate, never experimenting with the video/music combination. When *Fast Company* first debuted as a business magazine in 1995, it represented a dramatic shift from typical business publications. Everything about how the magazine was designed—the font, the artwork, and the layout—was different. Within six months, other business magazines were copying *Fast Company*'s format, and it became a leader in the industry. Brian Chesky, founder of Airbnb, intentionally set out

to challenge the status quo in a constructive way. Airbnb is now the largest accommodation provider, and yet they own no hotels and are slowing down the growth of hotel revenues.

Innovation requires disobedience. Unfortunately, you can't follow someone else's blueprint to innovate. As you look at the history of school reform, it is easy to see how many efforts have actually been copied from those creating change elsewhere, yet the results don't scale and have only led to small adjustments. It seems schools have mastered the art of incremental change, but these incremental changes have not gotten us to where we need to be. In fact, these incremental changes are likely to be obsolete over time. For years, we have been improving and changing educational systems and yet, in many ways, they remain largely the same.

Think back to your own educational experience as a student. Let's imagine it's the first day of 6th grade. You walk into your classroom wearing your new back-to-school outfit and carrying your backpack full of supplies. Sadly, you can pretty much predict how the day will go. Why? Because it will be like every other first day of school you have experienced. There will be some sort of get-to-know-you activity, the sorting of supplies, and the labeling and sectioning of binders. Then there's the passing out of textbooks and workbooks. In between, there are the rules: classroom rules, homework rules, hallway rules, playground rules. You quickly learn that school is a series of rules and events, all driven by the teacher, and you are just along for the ride.

When you were a teacher, you likely planned the first day of activities based largely on what you experienced as a student and acted in accordance with what you believed was expected of you. Now, as the educational leader, whether principal or superintendent, your first-day activities are likely dictated by past practices and perceived school and community expectations. In education, we take many things for granted and just assume "that's the way it has to be," because that is the way things have always been done.

As creatures of habit, we rely on our assumptions and past practices to guide most of what we do in a given day. We can reduce the amount of conscious thought required by relying on developed habits that help us accomplish all sorts of things. Put more simply, it is just plain easier to keep doing things the way we have always done them. This is true in both our professional and our personal lives.

Have you ever asked your child, "How was your day at school?" only to have them say, "Fine"? Alyssa became inspired by an article she read on Huffington Post, "Twenty-Five Ways to Ask Your Kid, 'So, How Was School Today?' Without Asking Them, 'So, How Was School Today?'" She was determined to change the daily conversation she had with her two school-age boys. So she armed herself with 25 new questions to ask them. The first day of her new mission went great. She asked both boys, "What word did your teacher use the most today?" and "Where were you the happiest today?" Surprisingly, both boys had stories to share, and she earned a new glimpse into their little worlds. You would think that this success would motivate her to continue with new questions, and yet the next day she found herself sitting in the carpool lane at school, both boys loaded into their booster seats, asking, "So, how was your day at school?" Habits can seem nearly impossible to break.

For most of us, the rituals and routines of schools have become well-established habits. We don't question them or expect school to be any different than it is—especially when we are talking about making changes to a system that so many of us are products of. Too often we hear, "I survived school . . . . It worked for me, what's wrong with it?" Yes, that system worked for us, too. Everything we needed for research could be found in the *Encyclopedia Britannica* and we relied heavily on our ability to memorize content. In this traditional system, we "learned" at school, and then we left to "do" at home. This approach no longer works. Learning and doing have become inseparable. If we continue with the same habits, are we preparing students for a world that no longer exists? Thankfully, habits can be broken. Old habits can be discarded and new habits created. As Charles Duhigg, the author of *The Power of Habit,* points out, "Once you understand that habits can change, you have the freedom and the responsibility to make them. Once you understand that habits can be rebuilt, the power becomes easier to grasp and the only option left is to get to work" (Duhigg, 2014, iBook Location p. 531).

What if by breaking rules with intention and rebuilding new habits, we were able to change the first-day experience for students? What if the first day was about the learner? What if teachers didn't explain the rules, but encouraged students to create them? What if, instead of handing out textbooks, students were handed an idea to explore or a problem to solve? What if students were encouraged to pursue topics that interested them? Or even better, what if teachers were encouraged to pursue "interesting"?

Breaking rules with intention is really a mindset of thoughtfully challenging the way we always do things. Some of these might be written rules, but more than likely, many may just be common practices that have existed at our school sites forever. Why do we require students to walk in straight lines? Why do we give spelling tests every Friday? Why do we use bells to signal time at schools? Why do we attend school for 180 days a year? Is that really the magic number of learning hours needed to master the content? Unfortunately, many of our accepted practices were created over the years for the convenience of the adults and have very little to do with what is best for students and learning. Some of these rules or practices may have been created for a good reason, but many have outgrown their usefulness. This is especially true when we consider how learning has changed over time. New skills are required of students; former constraints no longer apply or serve. The World Economic Forum released a report in January 2016 on the future of jobs that has indicated how important these new skills will be in the Fourth Industrial

Revolution: "Most existing education systems at all levels provide highly siloed training and continue a number of 20th century practices that are hindering progress on today's talent and labor market issues" (World Economic Forum, 2016c, p. 32).

The 10 Skills You Need to Thrive in the 4th Industrial Revolution, Alex Gray, World Economic Forum Report, 2016

In 2020	In 2015
1. Complex Problem Solving	1. Complex Problem Solving
2. Critical Thinking	2. Coordinating with Others
3. Creativity	3. People Management
4. People Management	4. Critical Thinking
5. Coordinating with Others	5. Negotiation
6. Emotional Intelligence	6. Quality Control
7. Judgment and Decision Making	7. Service Orientation
8. Service Orientation	8. Judgment and Decision Making
9. Negotiation	9. Active Listening
10. Cognitive Flexibility	10. Creativity

The world clearly has changed drastically, and yet many of our educational institutions are embracing practices of the past that have become so much a part of us, we no longer question why we do them. This is further exasperated by the fact that most of our teachers and parents are also a product of the educational system and, as a result, are accustomed to the routines, rules, and rituals of school. We are all fish swimming in the ocean, having a hard time describing what the water is like around us. And yet, in order to change practices, we must first become uncomfortable with the status quo.

Refuse to Accept the Status Quo

Rule Breakers dare to look beyond the status quo with a positive mindset, confident that they have other options available to them. Rule Breakers give you thoughtful headaches, as they don't accept the default options in life. For example, Adam Grant, author of *Originals,* uncovered some new insights about what your web browser says about you. When you purchase a computer, it comes with a default browser installed: Internet Explorer if you own a PC, Safari if you own a Mac. The actual browser you use doesn't matter; what does matter is how you acquired it. Sixty-seven percent of computer users stick with the default browser without ever questioning whether or not there is a better option. Those who select and download Chrome or Firefox display some initiative and take steps to personalize their browsing experience. Choosing the default system is certainly easier. It is a stance that says, "The world is supposed to be this way; therefore, I don't need to be dissatisfied with it." This default stance also keeps us from considering alternative and, in many cases, better solutions. What are the default settings at your school? Below are a few ways to move beyond the "default settings" of education.

Dare to Imagine

If you don't know what you could do if you could do whatever you wanted, then how on earth can you know what you would do under constraints?

—Russell Ackoff, pioneer of systems thinking

What is the biggest difference you could make? What would learning look like if you had no constraints? It is healthy to spend some time in the world of possibility. If we don't know what we would create without any constraints, then how can we create once we have the constraints? Spend a few minutes dreaming big and imagine what your school could be without any constraints or rules. Alyssa recently worked with an elementary school staff in Los Angeles helping them dream big, and it was important for us to play with possibilities. It is interesting to see how difficult this is for people. It took the team quite a while to suspend judgment and play, but eventually we played with ideas like "What if we created a makerspace in the middle of campus? What if every student had the luxury of spending time every day learning about something they loved? What if teachers had the ability to learn during their workday?" Once the team got rolling, they realized the possibilities were endless.

Stop Worrying About Being Right

As hard as it sounds, don't be afraid to let others be closer to the solution and final outcome. Position yourself within your community as a learner. With all the shifts happening, leaders no longer have to be the only experts. Embrace this. Be confident in what you do know and open yourself up to new possibilities by admitting you don't have all the answers. Shakespeare famously wrote: "The fool doth think he is wise, but the wise man knows himself to be a fool." It's human nature to want to be right. It feels good. It is validating, but at the end of the day, being a leader who is a learner and is able to suspend certainty feels even better than always being right. Try starting from the assumption that you don't know all the answers. The next time you are asked something you don't immediately know the answer to, try starting with, "I don't know . . . ." While working with one district on the exploration of competency models, not surprisingly, the question of age and grade levels surfaced. Do all students need to be grouped by age for their school day? As educational consultants, we certainly have our opinions; however, it was more powerful to respond, "I'm not sure, let's investigate." This simple shift—of not having the answers—allowed us to facilitate an exercise imagining "a day in the life of a student," exploring all the possible options and configurations of student groupings together. Had we offered an expert opinion, the conversation would have likely been much narrower in scope.

Take Inventory

When problem solving or designing, you have likely heard the phrase "think outside the box." Before you can effectively do that, you need to take careful inventory of what's in the box. There is a reason why the box exists, and understanding the current constraints that make the box function is key to knowing how to bend, break, or stretch those existing lines. Try setting some time aside each day to simply take notice of the rules, rituals, and routines that guide everything about your organization. Are they serving students well? Why do they exist? Who created them? What was the rationale for the genesis of the rule or practice? By starting to take inventory of these rules, you will gain greater understanding of how many daily practices and behaviors are ingrained. Armed with an inventory of rules, routines, and rituals, you are now ready to consider why these rules are in place and whether or not they should continue.

Don't Allow "Yeah, But . . . "

In this next phase of exploration, you will likely come face-to-face with many "yeah, buts." People don't necessarily like to question the rules they have come to embrace and may respond with "yeah, but . . ." if they feel pushed outside their comfort zones, want to justify their behavior, or want to avoid having to make any changes. It is a deceiving response, as the "yeah" makes it sound like there is agreement, but then the "but" negates any movement forward. How many times have you found yourself having a conversation that requires an openness to new ideas and new ways to do things, only to have the first response be "yeah, but . . ."? To help avoid this natural response, you may want to declare your staff meeting area as a "yeah, but . . ."–free zone. The simple act of calling out "yeah, but . . ." will help draw awareness to our reluctance to change and may help you instead create a culture where risk taking begins to feel more natural. Try to extinguish "yeah, but . . ." in conversations by offering replacement language instead. Challenge yourself and others to replace any "yeah, buts" with a simple, "yes, and . . ." (which allows you to build on the idea being offered) or a "what if?" (which allows you to question the idea that is being presented in a positive light).

Habits, constraints, lack of time, and fear of the unknown are all "yeah, buts," or common excuses that contribute to complacency in the way we do business in schools. "There just isn't enough time." "We don't have the budget for that." "It's too hard." "I don't know where to start." These reactions are not unique to education; they are common responses to change in general. They aren't just lame excuses, but powerful forces that we must understand if we are going to help our staffs turn "yeah, but . . ." into "yes, and . . . ." Our world is full of increasing constraints, driven by an overabundance of choices and connections, as well as a scarcity of time and resources. What if we were able to embrace constraints and allow these limitations to guide us to creative solutions? Constraints can actually be advantages in disguise. For more tips see "Turn a 'Yeah, But . . .' into a 'Yes, And . . .'" in the Appendix.

Adam Morgan and Mark Barden (2015) write in *A Beautiful Constraint:* "Ten years from now, we would like to search Google for a definition of constraint and see it include this: 'a limitation or defining parameter, often the stimulus to finding a better way of doing something'" (p. 10). Constraint-driven problem solving can lead to innovative solutions.

It is exciting to discover educational leaders who are actively turning "yeah, but . . ." into "yes, and . . . ." On our journey, we met leaders who aren't just challenging the status quo, they are intentionally breaking the rules and bringing along an army of teachers who feel empowered to do the same for their students.

Learn the rules like a pro, so you can break them like an artist.

—Pablo Picasso

Design 39: Poway Unified School District

When you arrive at Design 39, you can't help but be impressed by the building itself—a magnificent new multistory building in Poway, California—but the real *wow* happens inside. Sonya Wrisley, now retired, was the principal of Design 39, a K–8 public school of 860 students that opened in September 2014. While Sonya was always accessible, you would never find her in her office, as she didn't have one. The traditional principal's office was abandoned and replaced with collaborative meeting spaces to be used by any of the employees of Design 39. Use of space at Design 39 is one area where many "rules" are intentionally being broken. Learning spaces around campus are designed with what is best for students in mind first and, as a result, teachers don't have their own classrooms. Teachers may teach in a variety of classrooms within their pod, depending on the groupings of students within a multi-age span. Multiple teachers share a "Design Studio"—think collaborative office space—where they store their personal belongings and collaborate with their colleagues during planning time every morning from 7:45–8:45 a.m. Learning spaces are large, relatively uncluttered, and varied depending on the learning activity: large group spaces, interactive screens to display student work, makerspaces, and more. This redesign of space, combined with a new approach to scheduling, creates the opportunity for students at Design 39 to be truly immersed in what they are learning. The day is structured with fairly large chunks of uninterrupted instructional time. In the morning, students work on integrated learning of major content areas, such as language arts, math, and science, which they term "Awesome

Learning Time." After lunch, depending on the day, students work on an investigation, often math- or science-focused, followed by an hour of "Minds in Motion," a new take on PE. Picture kids doing Crossfit, dance, and basketball; it doesn't matter what class students choose, what matters is that they engage, get sweaty, and have fun! On opposite days, students are engaged in "Deep Dives." These are student-chosen areas of interest where students develop their learning plan and goals, which they then pitch to their teacher for approval. As one student said, "If it isn't deep enough, we're just asked to revise it and try again." Bells never disrupt learning; even body breaks, formally known as recess, are taken when it makes sense for that particular group of students. This type of schedule requires much more collaboration on the part of the adults at school; however, it results in a much better day-to-day learning experience for students.

Both space and schedules are big changes that can make a positive impact on students, but don't underestimate the impact of breaking other rules that may seem smaller. Believing that language matters, Sonya led the charge to rename various aspects of school, including commonly known locations and roles. "The School Office" was renamed "The Welcome Center," "Teachers" are referred to as "Learning Experience Designers," and "Noon Duty Aides" are called "Motion Managers." These may seem like small shifts, but they are intentional ones that communicate the beliefs of Design 39 and highlight how the language we choose contributes to the overall culture of the school.

Having the opportunity to challenge all the rules at once can be overwhelming, so don't underestimate the importance of challenging and questioning even the most basic of rules. Dr. Eric Chagala, founder and principal of Vista Innovation and Design Academy in Southern California, is actively building a school culture that encourages all learners, students, and teachers to push the boundaries, not for the sake of being a maverick, but for the sake of opening new doors and opportunities for learning. Eric understands the importance of creating a culture that supports this type of risk taking and models the behavior for others. There is an unspoken "rule" in education that educational leaders dress professionally, which for many male leaders means wearing a suit and tie Monday through Thursday. Most can get away with a more casual look on Fridays, especially if the school embraces school spirit days at the end of the week. No matter what day it is, you will never find Eric at school in a suit and tie. He has chosen to break this rule, as it signified a hierarchical organization and did little to foster the spirit of collaboration. Eric's attire most days is a polo shirt or school T-shirt, and reflects his belief in a flattened hierarchy. He feels more effective at getting into the real learning with the kids, alongside teachers. A colleague recently asked Eric, "How do the teachers and parents respect you in a serious situation if you are wearing jeans and a school T-shirt?" Eric's response to questioning the "unspoken rule" of dress is: "If it takes what I wear to garner respect in my community, then I have failed as a leader." This may not sound like a big rule to break, but it has helped Eric shape the type of learning community he hopes to foster.

Create a Culture of Inquiry and Innovation to Foster Rule Breaking

To move beyond the traditional practices at school, focus on creating a culture of inquiry. Following are a few strategies to expand your curiosity, start questioning, and create a culture of inquiry at your school.

Seek Surprise

Try something new in your personal life: discover a new type of food, read a book out of your normal genre, or take a new fitness class. Intentionally seeking out something new will not only help you break your routine, but also help you become more curious about the world around you. Knowing that people seek out surprises, Pack & Go, a travel experience planning company, offers surprise itineraries for brave travelers. It's pretty simple: you select your budget, answer a few questions so they can book the best experience for you, and then go somewhere. They do all the planning. All you need to do is show up and enjoy your vacation! What type of surprise learning itinerary could you create for your teachers? What if you queried teachers on topics of desired learning and then surprised different groups of teachers with a well-planned excursion that supported their learning? A middle school principal secured additional funding, asked teachers what topics they were interested in learning about, and then provided registrations to conferences that supported their learning goals.

Simple Change/Profound Impact

What is the simplest thing you can reimagine that will have the most profound impact? Is there something small, a practice or rule that has bothered you at your school? If so, investigate it using a simple one-two-three approach: (1) *identify* one simple rule or practice getting in your way, (2) *ask why* the rule or practice exists, and (3) *modify* the rule or practice to make a big impact. Ashley Auspelmyer, the lead teacher of Studio D, a school within a school at Westwood High School, ran into a challenge with the established hall pass rule. Not uncommonly, Westwood has a rule that states any student out of class must be in possession of a hall pass. As an interdisciplinary school, the expectation is that students are not limited to a classroom setting; they are out and about talking to people as a part of their learning. How could Studio D support this type of learning with only one hall pass for 116 students? After identifying the rule that was getting in the way of learning, Ashley printed 116 hall passes, one for every student in Studio D. In the future, Ashley hopes that this modification of the "hall pass rule" will lead to a culture change across the entire school, one that says we can trust our students to do the right thing.

Question Publicly

Create a public list of things you are curious about. What questions might make your top-10 list? Here are a few of the questions swirling in our minds as we begin to explore the future of learning for children:

- Why do we determine what a child learns and is exposed to based on how old they are?
- How can we design a system that embraces the fact that not everyone learns in the same way or at the same pace?
- What role does learning outside of traditional school "hours" and "walls" look like, and how can we partner to make sure we are expanding opportunities to learn, not limiting them?
- How can we reorganize our current resources (time, money, people, space) to shift our system now, rather than waiting for a full-scale, start-from-scratch redesign?

Once you have your list, share it with your staff via a whiteboard in the staff lounge or, if you're feeling even bolder, share your questions with your community in the school newsletter. Then get comfortable saying, "I don't know the answer; let's investigate."

Support Other Rule Breakers

Design 39 has been able to accomplish many changes by creating a climate that supports rule breaking, encouraging teachers to question everything and then supporting them in the process. With the daily encouragement from their principal, teachers are engaging in a very different way of planning and teaching. Most of the teaching staff had previous teaching experience at other schools, which is typically seen as an advantage, but experience can also be a challenge. Experienced teachers can unconsciously fall into comfortable traditions or patterns more easily.

It is clear that the entire staff is working with a lot of ambiguity; they are out on the leading edge, doing work that hasn't necessarily been done before in public education. It is uncomfortable but necessary for the staff, as they learn a different way to work. Leading author and business leader Liz Wiseman (Wiseman, Allen, & Foster, 2013) suggests, "We have to get comfortable asking people to be uncomfortable. Don't ask people to do more work, ask them to do harder work" (p. 72). It is clear that we, as educational leaders, are going to have to start asking our staff and faculty to do harder work as we intentionally challenge the way we have always done things. Following are a few ways to support Rule Breakers.

Give Permission to Experiment with Something New

Give explicit permission for others at your school to question and rattle the collective mindset. Teachers may experiment, but they are unlikely to challenge the status quo without the support of a school leader. Over time, many schools have actually bred a culture of powerlessness among the very people we need to change. To overcome this, permission must be given from the top. The Ministry of Education in Ontario, Canada, provided their districts with permission to question and innovate by acknowledging the changing landscape of education and being up-front about the messiness of the process. Leaders at the top acknowledged that change would be messy and encouraged others to jump in without waiting for the perfect answer. They created a culture of risk taking that gave employees permission to try new things. Organizations that allow employees to take risks push the boundaries of creativity and what is possible.

Be Explicit About What Outdated Practices Can Be Left Behind

Teachers want to follow rules because they want to do right by kids, which is why it is not uncommon to find teachers still following an edict or rule that was sent out via memo five years ago. In a school we once worked with, in the middle of a new math adoption, 2nd grade teachers expressed frustration with the daily timed math tests they were giving students. They didn't believe timed tests helped the students who needed extra practice. The element of time caused more frustration than necessary. When asked, "Why do you give these timed math facts tests?" all of the teachers referenced an e-mail from many years ago outlining this district requirement. No one at the district office recalls the memo; they would be surprised to know how adamantly teachers were following the outdated guidance they provided. Be explicit with your teachers about which rules they can stop following. In fact, let's take it a step further and have explicit conversations around expectations. Teachers should never need permission to

- Make the best instructional decisions for students in their class
- Be learners in front of their students
- Take risks that benefit students in their class
- Rethink the resources and strategies they are using to instruct students
- Ask administrators for support in providing for the needs of students
- Publish their work or their students' work to a wider audience

This is probably only the beginning of what could be a very long list, but you get the idea. What permissions do you need to give your teachers?

Create a Personal Flotation Device

With so much change at hand, people may need to have a "personal flotation device." This may be a personal practice that is perhaps not entirely in line with the new direction of learning, but one that is helping the teacher stay afloat for the time being. Personal flotation devices are only temporary, and they provide teachers with a way to say, "Hey, I'm working on this, but am not quite there yet." During Alyssa's first year as a principal, she allowed herself a number of personal flotation devices; one that stands out for her was the weekly school newsletter. The school secretary had been at the school for many years and had her systems of how things worked. Every Thursday, the *Bobcat News* went home as a hard copy in the student folders. Alyssa can still see the secretary sitting at her desk pulling out the folder of clip-art on Tuesdays, preparing the newsletter. This was definitely not how Alyssa wanted to communicate with her community, but she also knew it wasn't the most important change for her to make in her first year as principal. So, even though she recognized the practice wasn't in line with her style or beliefs, she allowed the practice to continue for the first part of the year. What is your personal flotation device?

Provide Air Cover

The idea of providing air cover comes from the military world. It essentially means that aircraft are used to provide protection for ground forces against possible enemy attacks. We interpret this to mean that when the ground troops are engaged in a difficult operation, aircraft fly above to make sure that their troops are safe. While they may not be physically attacked, those in our schools who are making changes can sometimes feel under attack from parents, the central office, or even, sadly, their colleagues. Once, when working with Megan, a new primary grade teacher, Kami chose to provide air cover for her from her colleagues. Megan was experienced in Readers' and Writers' Workshop, which was a very different model than the one being used by the other three teachers at the grade level. She was often "under attack" by her colleagues because she was doing things differently. Knowing that the workshop model was in line with the future direction of the school, Kami helped provide air cover by offering additional resources when needed, allowing her to deviate from some grade-level traditions and communicating to the parents on Megan's behalf in support of these changes. While only temporary, the air cover provided the teacher with a safe place to work, establish workshop routines, and feel grounded in why the workshop model was the best way to personalize reading and writing instruction for young readers. Within a few months, the teacher was ready to share with colleagues and no longer required air cover. We are not confident these changes would have taken place without Kami's help. Where can you provide air cover for those making changes at your school?

Remember the Importance of Unlearning

We often approach challenges wanting to know what we need to learn, but do we ever ask what we need to unlearn? On September 3, 1967, Swedish citizens switched from driving on the left side of the road to driving on the right. This is known as H-Day in Sweden. It was a massive overhaul of their driving infrastructure. Their neighboring countrymen were driving on the right, and many Swedish drivers were involved in accidents as they traveled across borders. The Swedish government put forth a proposal for switching to the public, who voted no, not wanting things to change. They were more comfortable sticking to what they were used to. The government decided to make the change anyway and moved forward with their plan. To foster a successful transition, the Swedish government created a department in charge of the transition that designed a marketing campaign with a special logo, gave away special prizes and products to promote the big change, and even held a songwriting contest to commemorate the event (which was won by the Telstars for their song "Stick to the Right, Svensson"). In the hours leading up to September 3, the roads were cleared so the final signs and traffic barriers could be moved. Sweden was ready for H-Day. At 5:40 a.m., it was announced on a loudspeaker: "Now is the time to change over!" What happened?

Gridlock! It was complete chaos. While people knew what they were supposed to be doing, they had not taken the time to recognize some of the habits and rules that they would need to unlearn. For some, the change came easily; for others, their brains and bodies reverted to what was known. A short period of confusion and unlearning occurred as people worked through the transition.

Breaking long-held rules, traditions, or habits that have been in place for a significant period of time can be daunting. Working to shift mindsets, habits, and entire systems can create a moment similar to what Sweden experienced on H-Day—people feel stuck. Unlearning needs to happen before there is new learning. In education, we have our own unlearning challenges. Teachers may need to unlearn their traditional roles in schools, students may need to unlearn what learning means, and leaders may need to unlearn the concept of failure. How might you approach unlearning?

Learn by Doing

We all spend lots of time in meetings talking about change, but the best way to effect change is to act. We need to learn by doing and put our ideas into action. By doing this, we actually create knowledge in context, making it easier to shift conversations based on the knowledge that has been gained. You begin to see areas where unlearning is needed and new learning is critical. Accomplishments become measures of quality that are feedback for your process. No learning journey follows a linear path, and those moments of losing ground are actually important moments of unlearning, which you can best experience through action.

Onjaleke Brown, principal of Dallas ISD's N.W. Harllee Early Childhood Center for pre-K and kindergarten, is challenging her staff to learn by doing and to unlearn commonly held "good practices" for students in primary grades. Brown, a self-proclaimed Rule Breaker, went so far as to dare her staff to get rid of all behavior charts. This wasn't always her orientation toward learning; in fact, back when she was a teacher, she had rules—too many rules, she will say. Rules like "Stay seated on your carpet squares. Be silent in the hallways with pointer fingers over your lips." And back then, like many teachers, she used a public behavior chart to let kids know whether they were acting "good" or "bad" each day. Brown says, "You hear 'learning' all around us, but we don't let them touch, we don't let them feel, we don't let them look. Keep your head straight. Don't turn around (Light, 2017)." But this isn't natural for children or adults, especially when we are learning. Teachers rose to Brown's challenge, but ditching their behavior charts was a scary move for some. Over time, teachers embraced her way of thinking. Their unlearning of past behavior allowed them the freedom to try new and different things. Although Onjaleke Brown transitioned from rule maker to Rule Breaker, she does still adhere to some rules. Her current rules look more like this: "Hallways don't have to be quiet, and lines don't have to be straight. Five hops on a trampoline will help kids release bursts of energy and return to class more focused. A few deep inhales and exhales can calm down rambunctious students. Teaching preK students to understand their emotions will help them later in life. Knowing all 160 kids' names and at least one thing about them builds a connection so they trust her and enjoy coming to school" (Light, 2017).

Both/And Thinking

Increasing student choice and voice in the classroom is becoming more mainstream; however, many times the choices are presented to students as an either/or, much like when we ask children, "Will you be taking a bath or a shower?" The variance between options is very narrow and, in both cases, they will be expected to use water, soap, and shampoo. So it's not really much of a choice. The educational equivalent for students is something like "You can either use a slide show, or you can make a poster for your presentation." There is some choice, but we are still narrowing the learning and creative options. We are reinforcing an either/or thinking process. Many innovations are a result of both/and thinking. Teachers at a middle school we once worked with were contemplating how to include computer programming into an already-full curriculum calendar. In many situations like this, either/or thinking prevails: something gets eliminated, and a new program is put in its place. The teachers decided to embrace both/and thinking. The Spanish teachers saw a way to incorporate Scratch computer programming into their curriculum. They changed the language in Scratch to Spanish. As the students learned to create scenes and characters within Scratch, all the speech bubbles and voiceovers were created in Spanish, requiring both written and verbal practice. Both/and thinking allows new connections to be made that produce different results. The next time you feel forced to make an either/or choice, see if you can apply both/and thinking. The results may surprise you.

Make Excellent Mistakes

Failures show opportunities. Unlearning is not about being right or wrong, but more about letting go of what we have already learned or acquired. It requires being open to new ways of thinking and exploring what lies underneath our judgment. So, while we talk a lot about embracing failures as part of a growth mindset, we need to identify those failures that are truly excellent mistakes. What's the difference? We all make mistakes, but most often, we quickly apologize, pick up the pieces, and move on, trying again or trying something different. Most of our reflection around our mistakes is focused on where we dropped the ball. Excellent mistakes give you bigger insights into the mindsets and habits of those making the change. The focus is more empathy based and may shine a light on past practices that we do not want to let go of. Excellent mistakes give everyone an opportunity to dig into their beliefs and judgments around the changes and open a conversation. Sometimes people aren't aware that they are holding onto something tightly until they hit a wall or gridlock, as in Sweden. That's often when they raise their red flags and say, "Wait! This is a mistake!" This is your opportunity to frame it as an excellent mistake. Dr. Samuel West, an organizational psychologist, feels it is so important to learn from our mistakes that he recently opened a Museum of Failure. "The purpose of the museum is to show that innovation requires failure," Dr. West said. "If we are afraid of failure, then we can't innovate." His hope in starting a museum focused on failures is "to encourage organizations to be better at learning from failures—not just ignoring them and pretending they never happened" (Skavlan, 2017).

Overall, the move to the right side of the road was the correct one for Sweden. The short time of confusion passed, accidents decreased, and people are now safer in all the neighboring countries. While it would have been wonderful for Sweden to have the support of its citizens throughout the change process, Swedish leaders had a much broader view of the impact of the new traffic system. They could see that the benefits of the decision would outweigh the struggles of the change for the country.

Albert Einstein is often noted as believing that we cannot solve our problems with the same thinking we used when we created them. When we move to break big rules for transformative change, we need to be conscious of our current mental models. The changes needed are not linear, and the key to new learning might be to unlearn the old.

How Do You Know What Rules to Break?

At first it might sound counterintuitive, but there are a few guidelines that will help you break rules successfully. As you think about rules, think about your values and how these core values and beliefs align to the rules you are challenging. If a gap between the two exists, it is likely a safe area to experiment.

It is also wise to assess the risk of the rule or practice that you are questioning. What happens if the rule disappears? What is the worst-case scenario? Playing out the extremes can help mitigate the risks and prepare you for the outcome. Another way to test the water is to simply engage the students in the conversation.

Engage students in identifying the rules, routines, and practices that interfere with their learning. It may sound crazy, but once students get past the silly first thoughts of adding more recess or allowing candy, they are actually pretty good judges of what interferes with learning. If they were in charge, what old rules might they get rid of? Why? Are there new rules they would create? If so, what are those rules? Challenge your student body organization to get on board questioning rules in the light of "student learning."

In the Los Altos School District, we created Student EdCon with the goal of increasing student voice and providing students with the opportunity to redesign learning. Students spent two days focused on the challenge of redesigning an aspect of learning at school using Design Thinking. Throughout these two days, students worked in small collaborative teams and were exposed to incredible speakers, who helped bring the Design Thinking process to life. Everyone involved with Student EdCon learned a ton. It is probably debatable who learned more, the students or our teacher facilitators. At the end of each day, we debriefed with our facilitators to share insights, learning, and thoughts on refinements. At the end of the first day, one of our teacher facilitators shared how amazed she was by the level of depth being contributed by students. They knew what "rules" were getting in the way of their learning. The overwhelming question by all was: "Why haven't we involved students in rethinking learning before?"

Rule-Breaking Education Organizations

Educational leaders aren't the only ones starting to break rules with intention; large organizations are also starting to embrace the notion that "educational rules" must be broken. Education Reimagined is a national group focused on creating a new paradigm for learning, no longer relying on the outdated rules. Simply put, Education Reimagined recognizes that the current educational system was designed in a different era and structured for a different society. Their vision is a call to action, not to tweak or modify the current system, but to create a drastically different paradigm of learning that will serve all children. They are connecting and supporting diverse groups of individuals that are breaking the current rules in education. Some of the rule-breaking pioneers include Big Picture Learning, Design 39 Campus, High Tech High, Iowa BIG, Lindsay Unified School District, MC2, Quest to Learn, Re-School Colorado, and Roycemore School. We encourage you to spend some time researching these and other schools that are further ahead in breaking the rules. Every time we read about their inspiring work, our reactions range from "Why didn't we think of that?" to "Ooooh, we could do that!" to "How in the world did they do that?" Fundamentally, our world is changing, and so should our education system. There is both comfort and power in knowing that we, as educational leaders, aren't going at this work alone. There has been a shift that is gaining momentum; we are confident that the momentum will only continue to grow.

Rule Breaker as Leader

Following all the rules leaves a completed checklist. Following your heart achieves a completed you.

—Ray A. Davis, author

Stepping into the role of Rule Breaker can be scary for leaders who are accustomed to playing it safe, but there are also huge rewards. With a little practice, Rule Breakers become happier taking risks and working out on the edge. They see the value of being bold, while remembering that bold scares people.

Jon Corippo, chief innovation officer of CUE, reflects back on a time early in his career when he chose the other path and how it made all the difference. In 1997, he welcomed his first class of students. He worked really hard, had a lot of fun, and had fidelity to the books that his district issued to him for his grade. His first year of teaching was also the first year of the California statewide assessment, and his scores were horrible. So horrible, in fact, he remembers them: only 24 percent of his students were proficient in reading. This was disturbing to Jon, who had taken a significant pay cut to "change the world" in public school. He felt that his plan was a failure. He started the next school year with a mixture of shock and deep reflection. His eureka moment was that he didn't really know how to teach reading, and he was simply going through the textbook he was given. He focused on improving his ability to teach reading independent of canned curriculum and began to craft lessons that met the needs of the learners in his classroom. He still consulted the textbook, but now considered it a guideline to be supplemented. When he received his scores the next year, 65 percent of the class was proficient in reading, leaps and bounds ahead of other teachers at the same grade level. He knew he was onto something. In Jon's fourth year of teaching, he switched from 5th grade to 8th grade and never received adopted materials for his self-contained classroom. He was thrilled and terrified, totally unbound and responsible in the fullest way possible for the learning of 27 students. Luckily, Jon had an ace up his sleeve. He had been building his own lessons based on student need for three years; this was just a chance to up his game. Many teachers embrace the rule of following the prescribed curriculum and march through the entire textbook without truly understanding the needs of their learners. Jon chose to break this rule and began to realize his full potential as a teacher.

Knowing that there are big challenges ahead for all educators and educational organizations, what rules are you starting to question? Let's stop tweaking our educational system around the edges and start intentionally breaking rules that will create space to reimagine school based on the needs of our students. Intentional rule breaking can help us step into the universe of possibility.

Chapter 6

Producer

A producer takes on any work that needs to get done
to move the project to the next phase.

—Lisa Kay Solomon, thought leader
in design innovation

If you have ever watched the Oscars and found yourself wondering, "Why don't the A-list celebrities accept the award for Best Picture?" you aren't alone. It can be easy to think that the Hollywood stars, the big names we know and love, should be front and center when collecting the awards. Yet the reality is that the film wouldn't have been made, much less be up for an award, without a quality producer and director.

A Producer plays a critical role in many industries, including music and film. In fact, without a producer, the latest film you watched or album you listened to wouldn't have been created. Producers are responsible for putting together a creative and talented cast and crew and all aspects of a film's production, including coming up with solutions on the spot. Producers must facilitate all the individual actions, then pull together the necessary components to deliver an outstanding performance. They are not only responsible for shipping a final product, they are responsible for all the iterations and pivots in the production cycle. Producers wear many hats. In the words of Hana Shimizu, executive producer, and Zack Kortright, head of business development for Hornet in New York: "Sometimes we are therapists, wranglers, negotiators, coaches, cheerleaders, translators, conflict resolution, bean counters, bad cop, paper pushers, spin doctors, food runners, naysayers, and problem solvers. The truth is, we are all those things and sometimes all in the span of a day" (Motionographer, 2017). Producers are the connective thread that moves a project forward from start to finish. They must also protect the line, which means staying true to the vision, working within constraints, and taking care of their talent.

Most of us have seen the movie classic *The Wizard of Oz*. During the production of that film, the original Tin Man, Buddy Ebsen, was hospitalized and had an iron lung put in after the powdered silver makeup coated his lungs. It took 12 weeks to get the dog, Toto, to follow actors down the yellow brick road, and the film changed directors five times. In the end, the producers were able to pull the production to completion and created a movie classic that debuted in 1939 and is still loved today. Producers must practice innovation and agile thinking at all times. In education, we need our leaders to embrace the talents of Producers, an idea shared by Lisa Kay Solomon (2015) in "The Rise of the Producer," to push learning from the industrial era into the innovation era.

Hustling and Looking Around Corners

Within one week, Alyssa had the opportunity to attend two very different education meetings. The first meeting she attended was at her local elementary school, as a parent representative on the curriculum committee. The group meets monthly with a set meeting time and vague directives. At this particular meeting, the committee gathered with a loose agenda focused on discussing whether or not Readers' and Writers' Workshop was the right direction for the school. Ideas were thrown around and discussions were had, but at the end of an hour there was no real clear plan for what would happen next. Two teachers even left prior to the meeting officially ending, as it had run over the allocated time. Thankfully, a teacher volunteered to arrange an informational learning session on Readers' and Writers' Workshop for the staff to see if there was broad interest, but it was clear that there was no real rush to get the information or to make a decision. Two days later, Alyssa found herself at another education-related meeting. This time the topic was much more global, focused on building a national grassroots campaign to provide tools and information for parents that would support them in demanding better performance from their local schools. The team was assembled from a cross-section of industries and, apart from this one face-to-face meeting for a few hours, they weren't geographically close to one another. All their future work together would happen remotely. This meeting felt very different from most education meetings. From the beginning, there was a clear bias toward action and a sense of urgency that underlined the importance of the work. Within the first hour, the group had clarified its purpose and created tangible action items with due dates and expected follow-ups. Alyssa left the meeting excited, inspired, and ready to take on big challenges. Having these two meetings so close together provided a clear comparison, and she couldn't help but wonder, "Why is there less hustle in education?"

Traditional education conditions students and teachers to wait. In a classroom, we ask students to wait to be called on, to wait for all the directions, and to wait for everyone to catch up to them. We train teachers to wait for the right curriculum, to wait for a district decision, and to wait for permission to try something new. While we encourage and instill wait time, hustle requires movement. Hustle has impact when it comes from the top. Creating a sense of urgency can be difficult in education, and the leader must show that change is *needed* and not just wanted. Oftentimes, educators and the general public use standardized test scores to make a success judgment. In schools that score well, with students measuring at or above average, complacency reigns. Why make changes when things are working? In his book *The End of Average: How to Succeed in a World That Values Sameness,* Todd Rose writes: "Most of us know intuitively that a score on a personality test, a rank on a standardized assessment, a grade-point average, or a rating on a performance review doesn't reflect you, or your child's, or your students', or your employees' abilities. Yet the concept of average as a yardstick for measuring individuals has been so thoroughly ingrained in our minds that we rarely question it seriously" (Goodreads, n.d.). This view of average, and the assumption that we are meeting the needs of the "average" student, leads to a total lack of urgency to correct any problems or make any significant changes. This lack of urgency may ultimately undermine public education as we know it.

Most of us remember the days of developing film, when Kodak was the go-to brand name for the film and paper you would trust with your memories. Even with the strong emotional connection Kodak had with its customers, they filed for bankruptcy in 2012, shifting from the world's largest film company to a has-been company beaten by the digital revolution. After 128 years of success, you would think they would have been positioned to "look around corners" and predict the innovations on the horizon. What you may not realize is that Kodak actually developed the world's first consumer digital camera in the early 1990s, but they couldn't get the approval to launch or sell it because of the organization's fear of the effects on the film market and their inability to hustle. They were worried that digital cameras would kill their film business, and they would have to hustle to promote the new digital way forward. So essentially, their true enemy came from within. Like Kodak, many schools are so inwardly focused that teachers are not aware of the changes happening in their own industry. While change in education is painfully slow, there are big shifts happening in the K–12 school space. Consider Alt School, "a partnership between educators, entrepreneurs, and engineers who are driven to deliver whole-child, personalized learning so that every child can reach their potential" or Big Picture Learning, an organization with the sole mission of putting students directly at the center of their own learning. Without the hustle and ability to look around the corners, are public schools in danger of going the way of Kodak?

School leaders who see the importance of hustle and looking around corners actively engage in behaviors that support these actions at their school site. They are aware that, at the end of the day, you need to get stuff done and deliver. All the talking and planning in the world doesn't matter if you don't ship something, which means there are times when you need to pull the lever and act. Eric Chagala, principal of Vista Innovation and Design Academy, experienced the lack of hustle in education firsthand when his entire district had been talking about implementing makerspaces at every school for months, with no action. Not one to wait around, Eric led his staff to learn about makerspaces and they grounded the experience in their why, planned training, and went for it—building the first makerspace in the district. Eric also hustled to get the staff to switch from rule-based to rubric-based grading. Eric admits it wasn't perfect, but he is able to help his staff see how their "bias to action" is helping them learn while doing. The school is in its third year of existence and its third iteration of grading. Eric's ability to hustle has led the teachers to act, learn, and iterate, a cycle that producers implement and replicate. Following are a few ways to provide hustle at your site.

Schedule a Wake-Up Call

Provide your teachers with a healthy dose of reality. Bring the outside in by showing them how fast the world is changing and what we need to prepare our students for. Once you truly understand the changes coming, you can't help but be intrigued by schools or districts that are making giant leaps ahead. Learn from these schools. Are you providing the same type of experiences at your school? If not, why not? Excuses aside, find a school to use as a benchmark, cross-pollinate, and start moving in that direction. Don't just limit yourself to schools; find ways to visit or bring experts from innovative businesses, design studios, architecture firms, and museums into your work. After each experience or interaction, ask the question, "What can we bring back from that visit or exchange that can inspire us to push further with our students or within our school?" One school we worked with reached out to alumni for their wake-up call. Through community connections, they were able to reach out to former students, many of whom had graduated college and were working in innovative companies, and invite them to reflect back on their learning experiences in school. What were the most powerful learning experiences? What did students wish they had more of in school? Every student who responded remembered learning experiences over textbook lessons, and all wished there had been more focus on how to work together to to solve problems and think outside the box, and increased opportunities to collaborate. Unsurprisingly, not one student cited lectures or content knowledge sharing as being instrumental in their current success.

Create a Ripple Effect

Remember that small steps lead to big changes. Challenge yourself to take one daily action that will get you and your school moving in the right direction. Share an article on student-centered learning with your school community. Try a Twitter chat (#dtk12chat, #edchat, and #leadupchat are worth checking out). Pose a provocative question to your staff. Challenge your teachers to do the same. Consider providing your teachers with a daily action that will slowly move your school or organization to a more student-centered learning experience.

Inspired to create more connected educators, Amy Romem, an elementary principal in Northern California, created a 20-day Twitter challenge, with one action every day for the staff. The daily asks weren't huge; they included actions such as sharing a book that inspires you, sharing a photo of the favorite part of your classroom, and introducing your colleagues to three new people on your personal learning network. All Tweets were shared using the #LASDpower hashtag. By the end of the challenge, not only had teachers built a more robust personal learning network, they had found new ideas and were inspired to continue the practice. The simple act of challenging her teachers to Tweet one thing daily led to much bigger results for their school—the biggest two being a dramatic increase in the amount of learning examples being shared publicly and the number of new possibilities teachers were now being exposed to. While Amy's intent was to challenge and inspire her staff, she reflects that the simple act of hosting the challenge pushed her beyond her comfort zone. During the challenge, she hosted her first Twitter chat, got skeptical teachers to join Twitter, and got a lot of positive feedback for validating teachers' work using social media. Amy said the experience was tiring, nerve-wracking, and totally invigorating, so much so that she can't wait to dream up the next challenge that will push both her and her staff. What daily action will you challenge your staff to take?

Look Around Corners

Become a student of the future and use this information to prepare you and your staff to be nimbler with the changes that are coming. There are publications and organizations that specialize in the future of learning. A few to check out include the

NMC Horizon Report, Institute for the Future, and Singularity Hub, but don't limit yourself to educational publications. Try reading *Harvard Business Review, Fortune, Inc., Wired,* and *Fast Company.* Could it really be that in just a decade, intelligent machines will have surpassed biological humans in almost every capacity? Read about the future you are preparing kids for. Find things that excite you about the future and bring back those things that give you energy. A positive future outlook is important, as the future is unlikely to be changed by people who aren't positive about it.

Once urgency has been established, Producers act. They ensure that everything they do and their team does moves them one step closer to the end goal. They jump in and go with the current, not allowing anxiety to paralyze them and prevent them from getting ready for the future. This isn't easy, but incorporating play helps. Play is one of the greatest cures for anxiety. One of the reasons design thinkers have embraced the tenets of improv, mentioned in Chapter 2, is that it allows your team to interact and be silly within a prescribed and safe space. We incorporate short improv games and activities throughout every workshop or professional development event that we lead and, although there may be a bit of eye rolling at the beginning, by the end you'll hear comments like, "I usually hate that stuff, but this was fun and I totally get why we do it." It's hard to worry when you are laughing and playing. Don't forget to play.

The Ultimate Power Switch

> *Little by little, a little becomes a lot.*
>
> —Tanzanian proverb

Producers are the ultimate power switches; they are constantly toggling between the big picture and the practicality of getting it all done. They work to make the impossible seem not only possible, but within reach. Donna Teuber, Innovation Program Designer in Richland School District Two, is constantly toggling between the big picture of scaling innovation across a large school district and the practicality of starting and supporting new learning at the teacher level, one team at a time. While toggling between the two can be challenging, Donna sees how each of the individual practical pieces start painting a picture when they are put together. It's not easy, but Donna believes that embracing the paradox between the big picture and the daily details contributes to long-term success.

Producers have the ability to zoom in and out, much like the wordless picture book of the same name, *Zoom,* by Istan Banyai. *Zoom* recreates the effect of a camera lens zooming out. The book begins with an illustration of a boy on a cruise ship, only to learn with a few zooms out that the ship the boy is standing on is actually an advertisement on the side of a bus. The perspective continues to recede, until the final picture shows a view of Earth from space. *Zoom* also highlights some of the challenges leaders face as they toggle between the up-close and big-picture views. When leaders zoom in, they get a close look at the details, but they may then be too close to make sense of them. When leaders zoom out, they are able to see the big picture, but they may miss some subtleties and nuances. Problems arise when leaders get stuck in either perspective. To be most effective, leaders need to zoom in *and* zoom out.

To improve your ability to operate as a Producer, analyze your ability to zoom. Where do you find yourself getting stuck—in the details or in the big picture? Figure 6.1 includes questions that may help you get unstuck and change your perspective.

Embrace the Paradox: Big Picture and Details

The most effective leaders are able to quickly toggle back and forth between the big picture and details, so how do you improve your own ability to do so? If you are constantly working in the day-to-day details, you may find yourself wondering how to

---

Figure 6.1

Perspective-Changing Questions

Too close; need to zoom out	Too far out; need to zoom in
• What is the context?	• What details matter most?
• What matters most?	• What are the most critical small steps to take to make progress on our vision?
• What is our purpose?	
• Where do we want to be in five years?	• What steps can I take to support someone (a teacher or leader) in moving forward?
• Does this fit the end goal?	

---

make sure you aren't losing sight of the big picture. If big-picture thinking comes more easily to you, you may need to spend some time zeroing in on the practicality of getting the work done. As you work through the "zooming" questions, consider allocating meaningful time to think through them. Too often, we expect ourselves to do the hard work on the fly and don't carve out time to think and reflect. Try setting aside some time to work through the perspective that doesn't come as naturally to you.

Build a Team

Another strength of Producers is their ability to put together a creative and talented cast and crew. They are able to do this by leveraging their network and the relationships they have built over time. Producers are relentless about putting together the best team and will work across all silos, even reaching outside the team to secure resources if necessary. When Alyssa was getting ready to launch a blended learning prototype in math using Khan Academy, she knew getting the right team together was critical for the success of the project. This wasn't a situation where she would be hiring a new team, but instead was looking to tap into the existing expertise within the school district. With blended learning being such a new strategy in education, she wasn't looking for teachers who had experience in these areas, but rather teachers who had the right mindsets, math teachers who were already questioning and experimenting with the best ways to meet the individual needs of their students. Alyssa was intentional in her choices, selecting three math teachers from three different schools, which would allow them to learn across sites and grade levels. All three of the teachers jumped at the opportunity to learn. The team met bi-monthly after school, but soon the three of them were meeting far more frequently, excited to share, compare notes, and learn from each other. The success of the initial blended learning pilot using Khan Academy was directly linked to the team that was identified for the project. We'll take a closer look at how to build your dream team in Chapter 8.

Create Rapid Learning Cycles

Producers are masters of creating rapid learning cycles for their teams. Because there is constant hustle and urgency, producers help their teams learn through quick and dirty prototyping of potential solutions. They are constantly cycling through the stages of prototyping, testing, and iterating. This runs counter to the culture in many schools, where the use of committees is prevalent. In committee culture, small groups are given a task and tend to work on it for an extended amount of time. Often, committees are created with a Noah's ark approach, making sure that there are two of each type of constituent represented (e.g., two teachers, two parents, two administrators), and in some cases committees are formed by including everyone who has a vested interest in protecting the status quo. Then, at the end of the designated time, typically a semester or a year, the committee unveils their solution to the problem they were solving. Unfortunately, at this point, each of the committee members is emotionally invested in the work they have done. While they may take feedback and tweak their solution slightly, it is unlikely that they will scrap their work based on feedback they receive. The way in which a Producer works is completely different. Once an idea is formed, a Producer may gather together a small group of people to quickly create a low-fidelity prototype that they could use to share their best thinking with others. They would then share the prototype with teams and users, asking for feedback. Because the prototype was thrown together quickly with their best thinking at the moment, they are not emotionally invested in the product. It is simply "Here is our best thinking; what might be improved?" At this stage, creators of an idea are more receptive to the feedback they may receive and will likely make changes based on that feedback. A Producer may take their team through this process several times until they get a solution that has received multiple rounds of feedback and is ready for implementation. Producers understand that part of prototyping is building to learn. If you are inspired to create rapid learning cycles for your team, school, or organization, following are two things to try.

Take a Break from Committees

In schools, committees tend to protect the status quo. Instead, think about creating Action Learning Teams that meet for a specific purpose, do their best thinking, and quickly get feedback from others. Not ready to go all the way and move away from committees? Then change their structure. Don't have committees meet for the entire semester or year; instead, have them meet as few times as possible to accomplish the task at hand. Encourage a bias toward action. The principal of a local elementary school was interested in creating a new vision for the school. With less than two months to go before the end of the year, the principal knew there wasn't enough time for the entire visioning process, but instead pulled together an "Action Learning Team" to do six weeks of need identification for the school. The group met weekly, had an intense learning cycle, and reported to the school's Governing Council with a list of prioritized needs and possible solutions. No, this didn't complete the visioning process, but it did establish a change in practice for the school: less talk, more action. The team was so energized by a quick learning cycle that produced results that many of the team members are asking to join the next group.

Increase Transparency

During times of change, organizations that have built a culture of openness fare better. It's easier for people to practice creativity and stay connected to the big picture when there is transparency. We have found, when working with teams in organizations that value open communication, people are less fearful of the unknown and more open to being transparent with their own work. It's really that simple. In the past, it was more challenging to be transparent with processes requiring lots of copies or additional work, but now, tools like Google Docs that facilitate sharing work invite people into the process. While working with the local elementary school's Action Learning Team mentioned above, we provided access to our work not only to the teachers but also to the entire community, by creating a shared doc that clearly outlined questions we were asking and linked current articles the group was reading. As a result, Alyssa found herself having conversations with other parents in the community while at T-ball practice or waiting in line at the grocery store. Parents were excited to learn alongside the school team and could more fully engage in school conversations as a result. What level of transparency are you comfortable with? How can you invite others to participate in your process?

Prototyping: Building to Learn

If a picture is worth a thousand words, then a prototype is worth a thousand meetings.

—Saying at IDEO

Put very simply, a prototype is a model that depicts a proposed idea or a solution. It is an opportunity to make the thinking behind an idea visible. Prototypes can take many forms—sketches, storyboards, pamphlets, digital mock-ups, and even role-plays can all serve as prototypes. Regardless of the form, prototypes make your thinking tangible. We will confess, the first time we encountered Design Thinking in the education space, we struggled with the notion of creating our solutions with pipe cleaners. It seemed way too simplistic for us, and it wasn't until we were outside of a workshop space with a contrived design challenge that we were able to experience the power and importance of prototyping. We aren't talking just pipe cleaners here; we are talking about the ways in which we test and iterate our ideas in real time. Several years ago, after attending Big Ideas Fest, we were inspired to create a three-day design-thinking experience for students. Having a hard time trying to explain the idea to colleagues who didn't share in our recent experience of attending Big Ideas Fest, we created a flyer for students detailing the "who, what, why, and where" of the experience. It wasn't perfect by any means, but the simple act of committing the ideas to paper in a format that was readily accessible by the user, in this case the students, allowed us to get very quick feedback. We quickly learned that students were very interested in the idea of the experience, but actually wanted more detail about the types of activities they would be involved in over the three days. We were able to incorporate this feedback into our second prototype, which we were now ready to share not only with students, but also with our administrative team at the district. After a few rounds of prototyping, we created the final flyer and launched Student EdCon—a three-day design-thinking experience where students learned the process while identifying and solving challenges within their community. Reflecting back, I am not sure Student EdCon would ever have been launched if we relied on discussions in meetings to propel the project forward.

Prototypes can be quick and rough. In fact, the level of fidelity of a prototype should match the level of thinking that has gone into the work. Think about that for a minute. Are you more likely to provide honest feedback to someone who presents you with a draft or to someone who presents you with a very slick digital solution? When prototypes are too polished, you run the risk that you aren't actually looking for feedback, you are looking for agreement. So don't worry about making prototypes beautiful; spend your time and energy making prototypes to communicate and learn.

Prototyping can also help alleviate analysis paralysis. Have you ever been in a meeting where a decision among several options can't be made? Prototyping just might be the answer for that. Instead of debating options to death, create quick prototypes of each option and take them out to your users. Get feedback on the prototypes. My guess is that you'll not only see which idea rises to the top, you'll also get suggestions to improve on all the ideas. As Tim Brown, founder of IDEO, says, "Prototypes slow us down to speed us up. By taking the time to prototype our ideas, we avoid costly mistakes, such as becoming too complex too early and sticking with a weak idea for too long" (Brown & Katz, 2011, p.105).

Pop-Ups as Prototypes

Pop-ups have become very popular recently, with more and more industries experimenting with this model to test or refine ideas. Pop-up shops, pop-up restaurants, and even pop-up museums are no longer uncommon in large cities. Pop-up experiences are growing in popularity because they allow retailers or chefs to connect directly with customers, build awareness, and test out new products or experiences. Over the summer, the Museum of Ice Cream, a pop-up museum experience, has become all the rage in Los Angeles. The Museum of Ice Cream describes itself as a "place where ideas are transformed into real experiences, a place where flavors are mysteries, toppings are toys, and sprinkles make the world a better place" (https://www.museumoficecream .com/about/). Originally only opening for two months, the Museum of Ice Cream had such high demand for their experience that they extended their timeline for an additional two months. What would it look like if you created a pop-up experience at your school? What would the demand for the experience be? How might you test out ideas in a pop-up model?

Identify a change that teachers or parents have been talking about at your school. Not ready to go all the way with the change? Try creating a pop-up prototype. Pop-up prototypes are wonderful because you can say, "We are interested in learning about this topic and are going to test out our solution for the next month. Let's see how much we can learn together." Setting it up as a temporary experience reduces the risk and may even encourage some naysayers to change their minds. Looking to create a makerspace, but not sure how the community will react? Try creating a pop-up Tinkering Club with community donations for a six-week period. Curious about a 3D printer or laser cutter? See if your school can demo one in a pop-up experience. Pop-up prototypes create an amazing way to make the learning process visible, increase transparency, and draw people in.

With a little imagination and very little cost, you can easily create a prototyping station—this might be a storage bin full of supplies or a corner in your faculty room. When staff members have ideas to solve problems, encourage them to make their ideas tangible and get feedback from others. Learn by building. For example, if a teacher has a new idea for a student summer learning experience, they could either create a brochure that might be sent home to parents explaining the experience or they might build a physical representation of that learning experience to show others. They might even encourage students to help prototype ideas. A list of tips and suggested starting supplies is included in the Appendix. *Warning*: once people become accustomed to prototyping ideas, the desire for prototyping corners across campus may increase.

Test and Iterate

The purpose of prototyping is to give you a physical model or experience that allows you to test and gather feedback. Testing out an idea can be as simple as sharing a rapidly made prototype with a small group or trying out a new schedule or strategy for an extended period of time. The most important piece of testing is the feedback process. In order to make changes to your idea, you need to know which parts of your prototype are meeting the needs of your people and which parts are not. Your feedback process needs to be transparent to those participating in the test process and easily and quickly gathered. Timeliness is key. A rapid iteration cycle can only happen if you are continually gathering information and data around your idea.

Practice giving and receiving feedback. Surprisingly, most of us are not great with either. When giving feedback, try this very simple yet effective prompt: "I like . . . I wish . . . what if . . . ?" "I like . . ." offers an opportunity to share something positive about the work you are providing feedback on. "I wish . . ." provides an opportunity to share an idea or suggestion for a future improvement, and "what if . . .?" offers an opportunity to share out-of-the-box thinking. This simple prompt can be used in a variety of situations: when presented with student work, at the end of a faculty meeting, or when providing feedback on a prototype. Try it! We think you will be amazed at the quality of feedback you receive with this simple structure. When receiving feedback, most of us naturally go into a defensive mode. Someone provides a suggestion, and we quickly want to defend why we didn't do that, why we were going to but ran out of time, or how that is actually included but they missed the feature. The true art of receiving feedback is just to take it all in and respond with a simple, "Thank you." Asking multiple people for feedback also helps you establish trends. Over time, people will see that you are receptive to their feedback and will be much more likely to share their true thoughts on any given topic or prototype.

Pivoting

Even with rapid learning cycles and prototypes, there may be times that you need to change direction, or pivot. In one of our all-time favorite *Friends* episodes, Ross asks Rachel and Chandler to help him move his new couch up several flights of stairs into his New York City apartment. As you can imagine, the moving doesn't go well, and every time they try to round a corner, Ross yells, "Pivot!," which indicates that it is time for them to change direction. You may find that there are times your team needs to pivot.

Pivoting can be tricky, but it isn't impossible. Often, the hardest part is having the mental fortitude to change. Pivoting doesn't mean failure; in fact, pivoting can be a great choice. It is unlikely that you have ever heard of Oden, a company that started out focused on podcasting but then chose to pivot when they saw iTunes cornering the podcasting market. Oden decided to pivot and focus instead on creating a microblogging platform that only allowed users 140 characters per update. You likely recognize this company. After their pivot, Oden became Twitter. It's not always clear; just because something isn't working now does not mean it won't work in the future. So how do you know if it's time to stay the course or pivot?

Consider the experience of a medium-sized school district we once worked with that was in the process of identifying and selecting a learning management system (LMS). The district put together a team to study options and select the best possible LMS to complement both their current student information system and the district's goals of personalizing learning for all students. After months of researching, the team made their selection, spent time onboarding with the LMS, and even invested in professional development with their teachers. There were some early warning signs that perhaps this wasn't the right option, but they chose to stay the course. The next fall, the warning signals became more visible when it was time to use the system for feedback and reporting to parents. Frustrations began mounting, and it became clear that this wasn't the right LMS for their district. It wasn't easy for district leadership to pivot away from the LMS after so much investment, but once the decision was made, the entire district rallied around the change in direction. Any progress lost was quickly regained as people felt thankful for the change in course. So what can propel the need to pivot?

You Learn More

It is entirely possible that a pivot is required simply because you have learned more, data tell you something different, or the conditions have changed, like a trip using GPS and Google Maps. Maps suggest a few routes, from which we typically select the fastest one available. Along the way, dependent on the driving conditions and data available, Maps will suggest better routes and reconfigure the directions. Sometimes new information helps us see an alternative route and recognize that a pivot is required.

Frustrations Are High

Listen to those closest to the work. We all know those people who constantly grumble; tune them out and listen to the others. Check in with your most engaged and open-minded teachers. Ask them about the initiative at hand and try to tease out the real concerns, apart from the more typical generic feedback, like "change is hard." After talking to enough people, see if you can establish enough of a trend that you can predict where you might be six months from now. Are you going to be able to alleviate frustrations, or will they mount over time?

Your Gut Is Telling You Something

In talking with leaders who have made a major pivot, they all expressed a sense of just "knowing it was the right thing to do." Trust your intuition. Sometimes we want to quiet our inner voice because it will require us to do things that are uncomfortable, but trust yourself. As long as you have your ear to the ground and are open to learning more, you'll know the right thing to do when the time comes.

Once the decision has been made to pivot and change course, don't look back. Pivoting can make you feel uneasy; it is natural to question yourself, but remember, the new path needs your full attention and support. Your team—whether that is school, district, or community—will likely have questions. Be patient with them; provide clear and transparent communication every step of the way. The district that pivoted mid–LMS implementation created extra opportunities for their teachers to express concerns and learn together to move forward. Fast-forward six months, and no one regrets the pivot.

Deliver

Finally, and most importantly, Producers deliver! They are deadline driven and understand that their reputation and resume are only as good as their last project. So while they are switching between those many hats, they continually have their eye on the finish line. Good Producers work to keep their values aligned with their vision and help everyone stay focused and collaborating toward an endgame. In education, we spend a lot of time on the process of change. Sometimes the changes that we have spent so long planning and implementing are outdated by the time we get them in place. Our current rate of change does not allow for this slow movement. We must become more agile in our processes and more focused on results.

Chapter 7

Storyteller

Every great leader is a great storyteller.

—Howard Gardner, psychologist,
Harvard University

There are two ways to share knowledge: you can push information out, or you can pull people in with a story. As a classroom teacher, one of the first things you learn in working with students is that story matters. Students have trouble remembering a list of facts written in their notebooks, but at the end of the year, they can retell in detail the story a teacher shared about a whitewater-rafting trip that included a fall out of the raft. Stories are sticky. They are one of the most effective and underutilized tools for learning.

As a leader, you are required to step into a storyteller role and, as with any skill, it is one that can be practiced and honed to inspire and create change. If no one tells the story, the story becomes lost. The efforts and progress that we made toward our shared goals and vision never happened. Without storytelling, our progress simply does not exist. As a leader at any level, it is within your power to craft and design the story that shapes your direction. You can inspire people and students to do great things, or you can zap the creativity and inspiration right out from under them. Storytelling is probably the most important and powerful tool that you have available. How you wield the tool greatly influences the outcome.

We are surrounded by stories, all being told in a variety of ways. Schools tell stories through newsletters, websites, and social media. We tell intentional and unintentional stories in our classrooms and in meetings. Every time we pull people together, we have an opportunity to build and tell a story.

Humans naturally create stories through experiences, and leaders can help shape the stories told. When leaders don't intentionally craft the vision or direction with story, we tell our own stories, filling in the missing pieces with our own interpretations, biases, perceptions, and experiences, which may lead us to different places. Think about the possible results of weaving stories into a traditional meeting. Crafting your story can help set a different tone and produce a different outcome. At your last district or staff meeting, were you listening? How engaged were you throughout the meeting? Did you leave the room feeling inspired, full of energy, and ready to explore a problem? Or did you leave feeling overwhelmed, frustrated, and disheartened because of the giant to-do list and confusion around the why? We could ask our students the same question about how they leave their classrooms at the end of the day. Intentional, thoughtful storytelling can make all the difference between these two outcomes.

Tell a New Narrative

The job of an educator is to teach students to see vitality in themselves.

—Joseph Campbell, American mythologist,
author, and lecturer

What makes a great story? What inspires the hero inside you to step forward and take notice? Great myths and stories have been used as teaching tools since people discovered language, partially because of the great power they hold. Stories have the power to pull you into adventures. They take you through the pain of loss, let you experience defeat, and most importantly, allow you to experience answering the call to adventure while helping you find the strength to rise after failure. You become the hero and carry those feelings of heroism with you, even after the story ends. It's why everyone loves a good book or a great movie. For a few hours, we lose ourselves in the life and adventures of someone else. We leave at the end having changed just a little, with new ideas and experiences that we didn't have before. Great stories make us feel, connect, and learn. Though not always apparent, the greatest stories have a similar structure supporting them. Understanding this structure and how a story is built can help you craft your own heroic story.

Joseph Campbell, an American mythologist and professor, is known for identifying "The Hero's Journey," a narrative pattern that is found in our most compelling and dramatic stories. Campbell's lifelong research helped uncover and identify common patterns that run through hero myths and stories from around the world. He defined several basic stages that almost every hero-quest goes through, no matter what culture the myth is a part of, which he calls "the monomyth." The hero travels from a known world through the unknown world, and returns to the known world having changed.

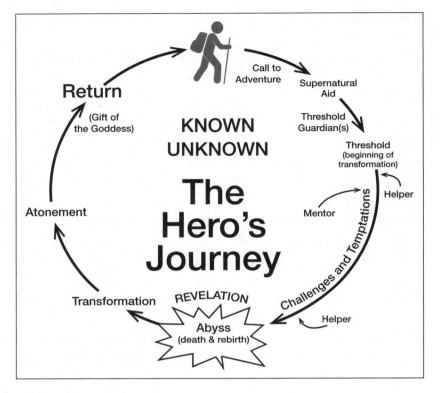

Beginning

The ordinary world. Heroes exist in a recognizable world, but often feel out of place with their current surroundings. They may be questioning the status quo, they may feel unfulfilled by their current work, or they may have unrecognized talents that they are unable to share.

Call to adventure. For heroes to begin their journeys, they must be called to leave their ordinary world. There is often some discovery, event, or danger that takes them from their ordinary path into a new world of adventure.

Refusal or acceptance. At this point, the hero must accept the challenge to travel or refuse to leave the familiar. Those who refuse to leave are usually met with consequences.

The arrival of a mentor or mentors. Every hero needs help and people to guide them along the way. There is often a timely arrival of support.

Middle

The unknown world. The hero is now headed into an unknown world with unpredictable outcomes.

Trials and failures. Our hero has many opportunities to learn and be tested, usually culminating in a final epic battle.

Growth. The hero grows in both skills and knowledge and, after the final battle, has a revelation that creates major change, transforming them into new thinking and being, which then produces a reward.

End

The known world. The hero returns home to the known world. Because the hero has changed, they return to change those around the hero, creating a better world and saving the day.

The hero's journey is important because of the commonalities discovered in stories across the globe. These are the stories that drive our societies and inspire change. The hero's journey is very much about humans and how we view the world.

Each of us wants to be a hero. We want the opportunity to travel through that epic journey of discovery. That's what makes learning so much fun. As leaders, we need to create our hero's story. Our teachers need that sense of urgency and call to action to create change in education. Our students need that sense of relevance and importance about what they are studying in their classrooms. As we start to put all our pieces together, we can craftily apply the hero's journey to create our collective story. Where are you on the journey?

If you look at the many initiatives and challenges that you face as an educational leader, can you define where you are in the story?

- Are you at the beginning? Your call to adventure might be that you're planning a one-to-one technology rollout, or you need to build community partnerships. Take a moment and think about which opportunities or needs are at the beginning phase. These initiatives will need a good why story, grounded in context and relevance.
- Have you already departed? Maybe you've secured funding and bought all those Chromebooks, but you're not sure how to deploy them. Maybe your school has embraced the idea and need of project-based learning, and you need to move it forward. This story is an action plan.
- Have you hit a crisis? Is the ship sinking? Perhaps your teachers are letting the Chromebooks sit in the carts at the back of the room, or there is student mayhem due to free rein on the Internet. This story carries a sense of urgency, acknowledgment of missteps, and a recovery plan.
- Success! You have arrived. Are you ready for the next phase? Where will this new practice or transformation take you? This story focuses on celebration and reflection that also allows you to continue looking forward.

Knowing where you are in your story can help you craft the right messages and deliver them at the right time.

Crafting Your Story

On a beautiful, sunny California day, we decided to hike up Temescal Canyon Trail for some inspiration. The trail is fairly steep, but takes you to the top of an amazing overlook, where you can see a good chunk of the Southern California coastline.

Breathtaking views. As we arrived at the top of the trail, we were quickly shepherded off the path by a young man with a camera and a large group of friends, who were clearly eager to surprise someone. Once we were out of the way, we noticed another young man toward the edge of the cliff. He was nicely dressed, standing on a white blanket set with red rose petals and champagne. Friends were crouched behind bushes and excitedly awaiting the arrival of someone. We deduced that a proposal was in the making. Sure enough, a young woman arrived with more friends, looking only slightly surprised; music started playing, and the man proceeded to get down on one knee, ring in hand, and ask the big question. She said yes.

As we watched this event unfold, it was interesting to note the number of cameras and the specific shots that were created to tell their story. After the proposal moment, the group went back and recreated different moments to echo views and to get just the right reactions on camera. They captured a photo with rose petals floating down around them, one with champagne corks erupting, one with everyone cheering. It was a genuine moment that was surrounded by production. Every element was clearly thought out, the experience was carefully architected, and many artifacts were collected for sharing and remembering. Within the hour, they had probably posted photos and a carefully edited video to a variety of social media sites. And if you hadn't been there, you may have imagined a very secluded and romantic moment that went perfectly. You wouldn't have thought about all that went into the creation of it. The storytelling work is likely invisible to most.

Social media has given all of us an opportunity to share every moment at the click of a button, essentially creating stories on the fly. People can achieve instant fame, either positive or negative, within a moment and the ease of a few clicks. Social media has also given us new ways to interpret the stories that we see and hear. Did it really happen if not fully documented on

Facebook, Snapchat, or Instagram? How are we documenting and telling our stories of learning in schools?

Before embarking on a new storytelling journey, you must first understand the current story being told at your school. Whether you are aware or not, every person who walks onto your campus or visits a classroom leaves with a story to be told about your school. This story comprises the actions of students and staff, overheard conversations, and artifacts, such as artwork and student work hanging on the walls. Everything taken in by the senses weaves together to create an impression and essentially become the story. Do you know what unintended stories your school or classroom might be telling?

Kami was in a classroom recently and noticed this sign posted on the teacher's desk: "If I'm talking, you should be taking notes." While we are guessing this was meant to be funny and there's probably a great background story that explains why it's there, to a casual observer, it sent a clear message of who was most important in the classroom.

We've walked around school campuses that were full of negative messages, where every classroom rule started with the word "Don't" and where most outdoor sign postings started with the word "No." Rules are certainly necessary, but how might we reframe them in a more positive context? A director of instructional Technology was reviewing their district's Acceptable Use Policy. It was a two-and-a-half-page document that parents review with their student at the beginning of the school year and then sign to show that they are aware of all of the school's technology use policies. It's comprehensive and important for online work with students; however, it was a bit language dense and written in a "thou shalt not" manner. Their team decided to create a classroom Digital Learning Pledge that was more positively worded. It was a short, one-page document that had statements such as, "At our school, we value communication and respect; therefore, I will use appropriate language in all my academic work and communication with others." Teachers were able to lead a discussion with students around expectations, and students were able to easily understand what was being asked of them, with the focus being on values that were important in their classrooms. It became more about how to build a community of responsible and respectful learning than a list of rules with consequences.

It's not uncommon to walk through elementary classrooms and see cookie-cutter projects that are almost identical lining the walls, except for an occasional crooked shape that a student was able to glue into place while the adult at the table was helping another student. While these "projects" are often cute, they show up every year like holiday decorations with little learning value. What story does this tell? Does it reflect and align with learning values? Artifacts are important to your story, as they capture a snapshot of your culture and reflect what's important to your story.

How might we evaluate our campus or classroom for its unintended stories? Following are two ways you might learn more about your current story.

Define Your Intention

What do you want to hear and see as you walk around your campus or listen to your students? If you could write a story about your district, school, or classroom, what would it be? Take a minute to sit and write or picture the story you want to tell. Define what students would be doing and saying. Think about what teachers are doing, and what parents might be saying in the hallways. Visualize your campus or your classroom. Know what your story should sound like, feel like, and look like.

Perform a Story Audit

Walk it. Take a purposeful walk through your learning spaces to see what artifacts are lining the walls. Better yet, invite someone from outside your school to take the walk with you. Walk with a parent. Walk with a student. Different perspectives will offer different points of view. They will often be able to notice more than you might, as we often miss things that we see every day and that have become part of our landscape. Note what evidence of learning you see. Can you see students' process as well as the end product? Is their thinking visible? Can you see individual students in their work? Pay attention to what posters are on the walls, what signs line your hallways or are posted outside on your buildings. Are they negatively worded? Do they encourage a positive culture? Do they reflect your vision and values? Do all the things you see tell your intentional story?

Talk it. As you walk through a classroom or school site, stop and ask for a story. Ask students to tell you about what they're learning—not what they're working on, but what they're learning. Ask teachers to tell you a story about the lesson they're currently teaching. Better yet, simply listen to the learning stories that teachers are using in classrooms. Are they inspiring learning? Ask a parent to tell you a story about their child at school. What are you hearing in their stories? Are their stories reflecting the culture you are building? What stories might you encounter that you didn't ask for? Some stories are crying out to be told. Listening carefully to the stories around you can give you insight.

Most schools run on tradition and habits, which often make those of us who are part of that story unaware of what it's become. We stop noticing the details of the world around us as we immerse ourselves in our environments. Our settings become familiar, and we are unable to clearly see the story that is being told. Stop and take notice. Audit your current story. By being aware and intentional in our storytelling, we are rescued from telling bad ones. (A story audit template and a template for the leaders' version are included in the Appendix.)

The Importance of Connection

The connection economy thrives on abundance. Connections create more connections. Trust creates more trust. Ideas create more ideas.

—Seth Godin, American author, entrepreneur,
marketer, and public speaker

Part of getting others to hear your call to adventure is first creating a culture that encourages the risk. Wanting to venture out into the unknown can make others feel nervous, confused, and fearful. Building connections with all stakeholders lessens the risk and is critical to taking others with you.

Creating a connection is often thought of as making an emotional connection or showing emotion, but it's really about making a human connection, one person to another. Our stories carry emotion and connect us through empathy. A well-told story gives us something that we take with us. Our social interactions are full of stories. When you meet a friend for coffee, you tell a story about what happened on your way there.

Sometimes, leaders are seen as unapproachable or disconnected from those around them. They may appear distant or unaware of others' realities and find difficulty creating connections with those they lead. During Kami's time in the classroom, she remembers all too well how teachers would talk about administrators as "having crossed over to the dark side." Once they stopped being in the classroom on a daily basis, they appeared to have lost their connection to and empathy for the daily struggles of teaching. As you move to an administrator role, your worldview suddenly shifts to a much larger picture, and the responsibilities of management become more focused on the day-to-day running of a larger organization. No longer responsible for a single classroom, you may lose sight of that experience.

How do you balance the big picture with the daily struggles of all your stakeholders?

Many leaders emphasize their strength, credentials, and competence in the workplace. However, those who project strength before creating trust risk eliciting fear, along with negative behaviors that undermine the organization. Leaders who work from a stance of "I know more than you, look what I've accomplished" often create an environment that produces parking-lot meetings, which are focused on complaints. Kami's high school calculus teacher spoke in a very loud voice. He had specific protocols for when you walked in the room: no talking, assigned seats, homework placed in a designated spot on your desk where he could walk by and check it off on his clipboard. He then lectured with a quick "Any questions?" moment, followed by an assignment. Questions were barely tolerated, and Kami was afraid to offer any new ideas or create outside of the structures that were given. When she walked through the doorway, her goal was to stay as inconspicuous as possible and survive the hour. She had a similar experience at her first real job. It was in an advertising agency, which was fueled by creativity, yet the leader believed that leadership strength meant he was always right and there was no room for discussion or ideas outside of his own. She lasted eight months before deciding that perhaps she had landed in the wrong career. Her creative confidence was down to zero. Fear undermines learning, creativity, and problem solving, often resulting in people getting stuck and disengaged.

Why does this matter, and how does it relate to storytelling? A leader can intentionally use story to create an open environment that allows others to grow and learn. Telling the story of struggle, challenge, and overcoming can connect you with staff, establish trust with them, validate their perspectives and feelings, and build relationships. It shows that you're not only strong, but also a friend, reassuring them that you're there to empower them to tackle any challenges that you may face together and do big things.

This connection with staff is so critical because, before anyone can decide what they think of your message, they decide what they think of you. By first showing a willingness to understand and share their worldview by sharing stories with them, you give them space to hear your version. Continue building on the exercises shared in Chapter 2 to further develop your empathy muscle. Finding balance in leadership, whether you're standing in front of 30 children or in front of 30 adults, is always a challenge. However, taking the time to connect with those around you and building trust will allow you to lead them to places you thought they might not go. Heroes need support. Establish your purpose, connect your team, and begin your journey.

Pull over Push

Branding and marketing are not traditionally thought of when we think about a school district or a classroom. In today's media-rich atmosphere, however, they are important elements to consider when building your story. Push-pull strategy is most commonly referred to as a marketing strategy. Think of pushing as the stick and pulling as the carrot. Pushing is setting something in front of someone and telling them they need to buy it now, while pulling is creating a need and building a relationship that brings people to your product and increases loyalty.

Many companies create a need for their product through a pull strategy. Apple is an excellent example. Apple has created a brand with a cool factor. Their advertisements are innovative and emotionally connect people to a want. Social media is highly utilized to create interest and curiosity, and speculation abounds over new features. People line up outside of Apple stores before the release of every new product, even though their current version of the same product may be working perfectly. They build brand loyalty that is almost legendary. Apple uses the power of social media to let customers tell stories that pull people to Apple products, causing a need to sleep on the sidewalk and be the first in line for a new iPhone.

We can harness that pull power in education. A high school district we once worked with was looking to add a learning management system (LMS) to upgrade their grading procedures and give parents more access to what was happening in classrooms. The challenge was that their teachers were not familiar with the features of an LMS and the potential it could offer. Their first view of a product left them overwhelmed and confused about the need for all those different elements. The report card and electronic grade book worked fine. Why should they change? The district stepped back and decided to focus their work around feedback. They brought teachers together to discuss the current report cards and the systems in place for parents to interact with student work and reports. They also began discussions around quality feedback and how it affects learning. Teachers started asking better questions and soon began asking for a better system. No longer were they overwhelmed by the idea of a learning management system; they were asking for one. They were ready to be pulled into a new process and eager to learn a new system.

The opposite of a pull strategy is a push strategy. Push marketing takes a product or service and places it directly in front of the customer, often at the point of purchase. It does not try to build relationships with customers, but looks for quick results. It's often used to introduce new products or services. For example, at E3, the video game industry's largest trade convention, Nintendo hired 250 brand ambassadors to work their booth, an aggressive strategy to place their games in front of consumers with a friendly face. A disadvantage of push marketing is that, due to the lack of relationship building, you must continually re-pitch your product to re-engage your customer. Nintendo may have gained some interest in their current product, but they will need to find a new strategy to sell the next one. When pushing an idea or a product, your story is less detailed and is continually changing to address the immediate needs right in front of you. In today's world, it feels like most of our time is spent learning something new. As school leaders, we often find ourselves at staff meetings "pushing" a new process: an additional need for more curriculum or a new requirement that is being mandated from the district office. We are often constrained to these strategies, due to our traditional time structures and organizational processes. When you continually use a push strategy, people begin to feel overwhelmed and frustrated, like they can't add "one more thing" to their plate. They lose sight of the overall vision and purpose, and it feels as if they are continually changing direction. Our stories explaining why we need this new thing lose their connections as we work to constantly re-engage our stakeholders.

What stories can we use to pull others into educational change? When we pull someone in, we use motivation, creating conditions that allow choice. We create a need so they can connect to the benefits of buying in, and we include them in the decision process. We create an authentic purpose and make it relevant. Carefully crafting a story around your new initiative can create a want, pulling others in your direction. Pulling may be more difficult, but it is more effective. When you push, you can't be sure which direction others will go; when you pull, you create the direction. Push and pull can work together. At times, we need to push people to break away from old habits. We need immediate results. This can cause people to be uncomfortable, so we need to be ready to pull them forward into our new way. The Next Generation Science Standards are currently being "pushed" out to teachers as a new national measure for what and how we teach students science. When they were first introduced, many educators panicked. The new standards were different, overwhelming, and confusing when compared to older science curriculums. Teachers began asking for a district-purchased curriculum they could implement. Due to the extensive changes to the long-standing science curriculum, there were no new products readily available, so districts have had to embrace a pull strategy. In one K–8 district we worked with, they began a slow introduction to the changes by modeling how to blend new practices into current instruction. They told the story of why new science practices were needed, and at every professional development event, they began introducing new ways to include science elements in every content area. Teachers experienced new approaches and were able to see the connection to more relevant and integrated learning experiences. They began reaching out to explore and create science learning experiences that embraced these new standards and practices. When asked if they were still interested in looking for a "science curriculum," they said no. They were comfortable designing integrated units on their own, and they could tell you the story of why.

To create buy-in and momentum for large change, our story-telling skills need to shine. When we carefully craft our story to pull people in, we create that demand. Finding a balance between pull and push is important for marketing and branding the changes ahead. Below are some ways to help you learn to pull.

Fine-Tune Your Call to Adventure

What is your hook? Most people don't want to leave the comfort and safety of their known world. Start by introducing new context that might cause those around you to revisit their current status quo. A principal who wants to question homework policies might start by bringing in the latest research on homework and leading a conversation around current practices and how they compare. What new questions might come up? Create importance. Allow team members to feel that their work will have impact. Whomever you're working with, give them a why that resonates and rings true, one that inspires them to jump in the boat with you and creates a sense of urgency for doing so.

Set Goals and Celebrate Small Victories

Most times, our vision and mission statements are big. We are hoping to accomplish big things and create big change. It's important to remember that not everyone can envision that high-reaching goal. We all know that taking a large job and chunking it into smaller pieces is the way to success, but at times we get caught up in the end goal and forget to celebrate the small steps we've made so far. Make them visible. These are the trials and failures during the middle journey of our story. Everyone on your team needs to be able to see and share in the small wins as they add them to their own story.

Let Them Drive

How often have you worked with a group leader who continues to monopolize the conversation, the pace, and the direction? You sometimes wonder why they formed a team to begin with. They appear as the only hero in the story and seem to need no support to save the day. In order for others to experience the lows and celebrate the wins, they need to feel like they contributed. They had a role and can claim ownership in the creation of the end product. In leadership roles, it can be hard to step back, quietly observe, and just listen, but these can be important moments. Learn about your team members. Understand their strengths and listen for their passions. You will be more effective when you step back in to give guidance and can empower those team members more effectively. Everyone needs to feel like they are taking part in the story.

Amplify the Good

So often when we head into problem solving, we start with an attitude of scarcity. We look at all the things we don't have and all of the things that aren't working. We enter problem-solving mode, and our first step is to look at all the negative shortfalls contributing to the issue. Take a moment to stop and recognize where you see abundance or things that are positive as you define needs. It's human nature to focus on what needs to be fixed, and almost always there are things among the broken that still work. Our world is constantly pointing out what we're lacking, what we need, and why what we have isn't enough. As you move forward in your work, it's important to amplify not just your small wins, but where you see things that are good. Help others see them and appreciate those who are striving to bring positive change and amazing learning experiences to our students.

All these practices can help you pull people into your story rather than push your ideas at them. They are invitations to join you on your big adventure.

Power in Pictures

We first learn to read by connecting text to pictures. Our brains are wired for visual information. Much of our sensory cortex is devoted to processing visuals, and a large body of research indicates that visual cues help us remember and retrieve information. Words are more abstract and difficult to retain, while visuals are more concrete. We have friends who can rattle off movie quotes from films they saw five years ago, but can't tell you much about the book they read last month. Visual storytelling is sticky.

In education, we use visual learning strategies to teach in our classrooms, but often we don't put the power of pictures into play in our other work. In fact, we tend to get a bit lazy with our language, making it difficult to share our stories in a way that communicates clearly. Kami overheard this conversation in the hallway outside of her office:

"'Do you have the information for DLT?"

"Do you mean the feedback we gathered around PLC work from CCCLT or the upcoming schedule of PD that we discussed at IS?"

We talk in code. In fact, when Kami first started working in a new school district, she was given a three-page handout of all the acronyms unique to that district. She kept it nearby for easy reference.

We also use what we call "edu-speak," language that is made up of popular clichés and jargon. Have you heard about data-driven schools closing the achievement gap through professional learning communities to create a new paradigm? ScienceGeek.net has developed a tool in the form of a word generator to help educators write reports or documents related to public school, boasting, "Amaze your colleagues with finely crafted phrases of educational nonsense!" The site has become so popular that teachers were creating bingo cards to use during staff meetings. ScienceGeek.net responded and added "Edubabble Bingo!" which provides randomized bingo cards and also allows you to add your own favorite phrases. Their argument for teachers getting caught playing: "Edubabble Bingo is an engagement strategy supported by current brain research on bored adults! Win!" Every profession comes with its own common phrases, and while the language sounds very professional and the intent is purposeful, in common conversations we can lose the emotion and the connection to the most important parts of our story, which should be more human-centered around our students.

Misuse or overuse of data can be another barrier to more effective messaging. Our public education systems are judged and held up in their communities based on test scores. Accountability requires that school districts file state reports that are full of data points and percentages, and while data are important to what we do and a needed requirement of accountability, they are often communicated poorly. Numbers given with little context can be made to mean many things, and we often hear data delivered in a defensive manner with a mix of different reasons explaining the why. This is not unique to education, but is a common issue with any industry that is difficult to quantify through just numbers. We deal with people. We don't create products, and our profits and losses are not always that easy to see or measure.

Our messaging around our visions—for what we want to create or change as we build new learning experiences—needs to be clearly understood by all our stakeholders, not riddled with poorly explained numbers and data points and bewildering jargon. So how might you work to show as well as tell?

How can simple pictures help solve complex problems? When we talk about data, adding simple graphics to help others understand and see the story of data is important. Today's media is full of infographics. Infographics have become a popular way to tell a story about many sorts of data. There are many tools, such as Canva, Easel.ly, or Piktochart, that make creating an infographic fairly easy. Because visuals are more easily and quickly processed in the brain than words, an infographic can transform complex information into pictures that are both easy to grasp and visually appealing. They allow you to creatively craft the story you want to tell with your data. Working in instructional technology, we have found infographics to be a great way to report and share information about technology usage, along with information regarding student and teacher skills. After using a survey tool to gather information around technology usage and habits, Kami was able to create a simple infographic that compared big ideas. It helped her highlight some obvious needs, as well as some numbers to celebrate. She didn't need to roll out all the detailed survey data; she wanted an easily understood visual that pulled attention to some big data points that supported the story of where they were going next with technology.

Assembling the Story: Putting It All Together

An important leverage point for transforming our education system is changing the mindset that gave rise to it in the first place.

—Todd Rose, *The End of Average*

21st Century Students and Teachers

Key Survey Takeaways, 2017

Foundational Skills

 24% 63%

Online Skills

34% 54%

Multimedia Skills

71% 48%

Digital Citizenship

10% 27%

Confidence with New Tools

| 48% can solve their own tech problems | 77% can solve their own tech problems |
| 90% learn from new technologies daily | 72% learn from new technologies daily |

Our story must be heard by all of our community. The first letter that goes home in the summer to welcome your students and parents to your school is one of your earliest opportunities for establishing your story. It is an opportunity to share your vision as a call to adventure. If your back-to-school newsletter contains only lists and schedules and rules, your story is a dry documentary, full of what may be needed, but boring. If we are working to change traditional education, what is our "new learning in schools" narrative? How do we artfully craft that story? Let's go back to Joseph Campbell's "Hero's Journey."

Beginning

The ordinary world. This is your moment to ask, "Do I want to create change or do I want to keep everything the same?" If you are happy with the status quo, then there is no need for you to move forward or to be reading this book. However, if we have had some impact on your thinking so far, we hope you see a reason to explore, to leave the ordinary path for a new world of adventure. You must decide. Are you feeling out of place? Is the work you're doing in education feeling disconnected from the world around you? If so, sound the call.

- *Give them a reason for change.* Build context around the need for change. Look for opportunities in your newsletters, in your staff presentations, and in your daily conversations to add information that reflects change in the world around us and that has an impact on how we educate children. Become an Opportunity Seeker and Experience Architect. Create a strong why, one that is clearly visible.

- *Create a vision pitch.* This is a short, well-worded pitch that you can give to anyone, anywhere, in a matter of minutes. Focus on your big ideas. One way to start is to think of a headline. If you were writing a front-page story, what headline would you lead with? What picture might you include, and what would the caption read? When looking at your big ideas, is there one that is a priority, one that carries a sense of urgency or will connect with all your stakeholders emotionally? With a vision pitch, you want to capture hearts as well as minds. If it's a solution to a problem, use facts and real examples to support your idea and remind people what's wrong with the status quo. You might draft a vision pitch like this:

— *Big Idea: Family Learning Nights.* Parents invited to interact with students and give feedback on learning projects. This could also provide opportunities for students to teach and share knowledge. Currently we offer no consistent way for parents and the community to be involved in student learning.

— *Pitch Points:*

- Headline: Community Makes Us Strong

- We believe students are curious and creative learners who succeed through personal initiative, sustained effort, and collaboration around authentic and relevant learning projects.

- We believe families are integral to the success of our students and our school.

- This could open up many possibilities for sharing and collaborating to strengthen our learning communities.

For additional practice, try the story frame in the Appendix.

- *Expect resistance.* Not everyone will answer the call. Some will refuse. Put your empathy skills and practices to work to learn as much as you can about the needs of those around you, not just to design a better direction toward a solution or positive change, but to figure out the cause of any pushback and how you might address your approach and messaging. Look for ways that your new direction will help answer those needs. Provide encouragement, guidance, and support where and when you can. If some choose not to answer, be patient with them. Acknowledge their resistance, but continue to move forward, circling back to continually extend the invitation to join.

Middle

The unknown world. This is where it gets messy. The process of change is not linear, and there is no road map. People will question your leadership and your direction, and it's easy to get stuck in the weeds. Those around you will feel uncomfortable and want to stay mired in the debate of small details. When you are in the middle of the story, it is important to stay focused on your bigger picture. Thinking back to our work together with LASD, we were focused on "Revolutionizing Learning for All Students," and we believed an essential component of our plan was to empower our teachers to be professionals and encourage them to do the best for the learners in their classroom. This was the opposite of a top-down change approach. It was fuzzy and ambiguous. There were times teachers just wanted to be told what to do. We resisted and held firm to the idea that meeting all student needs required multiple solutions, many of which would be developed by teachers. Whenever teachers got uneasy, we reminded them of the big picture, found ways to thank them for their innovative ideas, and provided additional supports to develop classroom-based solutions. We also asked teachers to share their experiences on this journey. Here are a few comments from teachers that encouraged us to stay the course:

> "Innovation to me is trying something new and then evaluating. It's about stepping out of my comfort zone and taking time for reflection."

"Being honest with students and colleagues about our own learning and risk taking helps them do the same."

"Biggest takeaway so far—divergent thinking, habitudes, and team building all more important than the tech piece of revolutionizing."

"Students have the ability to detect when your heart isn't into your lesson. Create new approaches to your low-interest lessons."

- *The design-thinking process is about iteration.* We prototype an idea and then use our empathy skills to gather feedback to see how we can improve what we created to better meet people's needs. Most likely, change will not roll out smoothly or be perfect the first time out. Growth mindset is a must. Transformation requires new thinking, and that takes time. Be sure to communicate this to your team. Remind them that it's okay for things to be a bit messy as you work through the iteration process.

- *The middle is also a place to practice some intentional rule breaking.* We can't reach a new destination without pioneering our way through the unknown. Ditch some habits and try on some new ones. You may find a better fit, or you may need to adjust and move backwards a bit to slightly change direction.

- *Return to your vision.* Keeping your big picture in mind will help you reorient as you get lost in the tall grass or the forest. If the conversations or the current work you are caught up in are not relating to your beliefs about learning and the values you have defined, pivot and find where the work matters. Continuing to tell your story is a way to remind others of where they are headed.

End

The known world. At the end of the journey, the hero and company return to their known world. Perhaps the world has changed, but ultimately, it's the people who have changed, impacting their old environment. Your journey has brought you to new realizations and new practices that create innovation. Again, amplify the good as you continue to tell your story. Your adventure is not truly over. This is an opportunity to reflect and think about the transformation that has occurred. It is also a time to use messaging to get feedback from stakeholders to help you look at what comes next. How can you leverage what you've just gained to go even further?

Who Will Tell Your Story?

Probably the most important part of a story is the delivery. We want to share our stories, and we want others to connect and share in our journey. The stories that are being told will build and shape your community. Look for opportunities to endorse channels of communication that allow your stakeholders to share and contribute. Here are some ideas for creating those channels and encouraging others to share.

Create a Facebook page, grab a Twitter handle, post pictures on Instagram. This is how we communicate today. We like and share and post. If you are not comfortable with these tools, look for others that might offer similar experiences, or better yet, find someone who is using them well and ask them to teach you more. Part of why we are afraid to venture into social media is because we see so many people using it badly. As educators, we have a responsibility to help young people become better communicators through these social channels. They will continue to change and grow, and we must help our students become digital citizens who understand all the moral and complicated decisions that come with unlimited access. How do you boost your social media savvy?

Hashtags

When posting online, it's common to use a hashtag (#), which "tags" your post and makes it searchable within a site. Most districts choose a Twitter handle (your @xxx Twitter name) along with a hashtag that will identify them within a post. For example, behind @campbellusd you will find the Campbell Union School District, along with the #campbellusd and #cusdrockstar hashtags. The rockstar hashtag is primarily used for teachers to share what's happening in their classrooms as well as knowledge around new tools and strategies that they are learning, both outside and inside the district. The hashtag #knowmystory is a great example of a Twitter hashtag that provides social posts of both teachers and students sharing and reflecting as they practice empathy.

Branding Guides

Community Consolidated School District 59 (CCSD59) is a district that has done an amazing job with their story. They have developed a branding guide that states, "Our brand is not a logo. Our brand is the district's reputation for preparing students to be successful for life. Our brand is the students we educate and the teachers who educate them." Within their branding guide, you will find an explanation of their logo, all the graphics and colors that are acceptable for use, and a guide for how photos and images should be used. They even go so far as to share thoughts on how pictures should be taken, citing this advice: "Perspective is everything. Taking photos from a student or teacher's vantage point is paramount. Do not look down on a student." Also, every month they celebrate a staff member through the "59 in :59" video project. It's their way to tell the story of the work they are doing to prepare students for success and build community through

empathy. You can visit the entire branding guide at www.ccsd59
.org/wp-content/uploads/2014/08/Brand-Guide-Web.pdf.

Build Learning Communities

Social media is a place where many educators go to learn.
Through Twitter chats, Facebook, Google groups, or Slack
teams, teachers are sharing their voices and creating leadership opportunities while connecting with others across oceans.
Using hashtags and following each other's posts, teachers have
developed a worldwide network that reaches far and wide. If you
want to join an already established professional learning network
(PLN), take a look at The Educator's PLN (http://edupln.ning.
com/) or Classroom 2.0 (www.classroom20.com/). Educators
are telling their classroom stories and finding ways to include
student voices as well.

Parent Voices

How can parents become powerful allies in our work? In a
recent visit to Design39 in the Poway District, the principal, Joe
Erpelding, shared some of the work being done to bring parents
together and help tell the unique story of D39:

- *Dine and dialogue.* Holding community dinner meetings
  allows the D39 parents to come together with staff and
  students to create an experience that allows families to feel
  connected.
- *Parent mentor program.* At D39, they are pairing up parents
  who have experience within the community with families
  new to the area. Because they have a unique program that
  offers a nontraditional school experience, having a parent
  who is familiar with their vision, values, and processes can
  help guide a new family through the unfamiliar.
- *Parent workshops or focus groups.* Parent workshops
  or focus groups can be powerful ways to bring parents
  together to learn more about the work you are doing.

Offering parents a way to have input and discuss how feedback is presented on student learning can enrich these interactions. Bringing parents in on discussions around changing homework practices or other new learning strategies can create a partnership and broader community of learning. We worked with one district on developing a strategic plan, and the district leadership was very open to including parent feedback. We hosted parent focus-group meetings around the future of learning, during which we provided thought-provoking articles and videos to stimulate thinking and conversations. We then asked parents to provide feedback to a series of prompts, which included the following:

—I wish my student . . .

—What if my student were able to . . .

—When my student graduates, they need to be able to . . .

After a series of these focus groups, we collected hundreds of ideas from the community that were closely aligned with the vision and direction of the district. The superintendent was then able to turn around and say, "This is what we heard from you. Our collective vision is . . . ."

Student Voices

Aside from creating a different classroom experience that students can talk about, there are ways you can enlist students' help in telling your story:

- *Digital portfolios.* Digital portfolios offer a way for students to have a visual reference for their work and verbally reflect and comment on their learning. Over time, they accumulate a story that represents their learning journey. Tools like Seesaw allow students to share and comment on each other's work, practicing those digital citizenship skills, and also can give parents a window into the classroom so they can see and comment on the story of their child's school day.

- *Students on Periscope.* At Design 39, they occasionally invite a student to use a digital device to tour the school and give a narrative of what's happening that day. They promote this event through their social media channels, and parents can't wait to tune in to Periscope to see what's happening live on campus.

The stories we tell ourselves and the stories we tell each other will come in many shapes and sizes, but they should carry the same overall feeling and message. So dig in, hone your storytelling skills, and round up your storytellers! Along the way, ask yourself if you all are aligned and telling the same story and, most importantly, if you are all telling an exciting story you can be proud of.

Chapter 8

Design Your Team and Your Mindset

Alone we can do so little, together we can do so much.

—Helen Keller

If you are feeling a little overwhelmed by the five new roles, take a deep breath and think about what an incredible opportunity you have to design both your team and your mindset. While the heroic leader who takes on the work solo is often celebrated, and we hear stories of leaders confronting challenges with single straight lines to amazing and innovative solutions, we believe leadership is much more complex. The line from challenge to solution won't be straight, and the work won't be done solo, because design-inspired leadership practiced by a team will have the greatest positive impact on changes in our school system. It's not really surprising that most heroic work or discoveries are actually made by teams, not solo leaders. Studies show that people working in teams tend to achieve better results and report higher job satisfaction. No team can survive on the brainpower or work of one person. Design Thinking is a team sport that requires the involvement of every member on the team, and design-inspired leaders know how to harness and utilize that energy.

Design Your Team

Design Thinking not only fosters innovation, it also strengthens teams by creating common language, common artifacts, and a culture that is built on trust. It is not uncommon for teams to have different interpretations of the same idea or goal. Building a shared language helps teams move from figuring out the "what" to figuring out the "how." The creation of artifacts happens throughout the design process, which is so powerful because it requires people to "show rather than tell" through empathy maps, storyboards, and walls full of ideas written on sticky notes. The visualization of complex ideas actually helps the team simplify ideas, making it more likely the team will move to action. The practice of Design Thinking helps build trust across a team, as all ideas carry equal weight no matter whom they came from. While the main goal of Design Thinking is to create solutions to wicked problems, one of the benefits of engaging in the design process is that it also builds strong teams by helping establish the climate of collaboration, risk taking, and trust that will lead to high-performing teams. The simple act of choosing to engage in the design process will result in a stronger, more effective team.

So how do you design and build the perfect team? Google, looking to optimize their teams, set out to answer that question in 2012 with "Project Aristotle." The group—comprising statisticians, organizational psychologists, sociologists, engineers, and researchers—was tasked with researching and identifying the qualities that make up the best and most effective team. They started with research and academic studies, but then moved on to researching hundreds of teams, scrutinizing every aspect of them. Do the best teams socialize outside work? Do they have similar interests? How does gender balance impact the team? Does a team need to have similar educational backgrounds? The list of factors they researched was extensive, but in the end, they discovered there is no such thing as creating the perfect team. Teams that are successful are successful because of the ways they have chosen to work together. The team's norms are a greater predictor of success than the actual composition of the team. So in some regards, it is less about who is on the team and more about the ways in which members interact with one another.

In their simplest form, norms are informal understandings that govern the behavior of members of a group. Norms can be unspoken or explicitly expressed; either way, they have profound influence over how a team works together. Individuals on a team may behave in certain ways when alone, but when they are together, the group's norms typically override any one individual's preferences or proclivities. It would be easy to think, "Problem solved! We'll create one set of norms and have those govern every team." Not so fast. The norms have to be created and enforced by the group as they work together. Even if a team sets out to develop norms explicitly, these norms will organically change over time based on the will of the team. Project Aristotle took their research one step further to see if they could identify any common norms in successful teams. The norms varied from team to team, but they did find two common threads in all successful teams. Successful teams all had "equality in distribution of conversational turn taking" and "average social sensitivity," which means that team members were empathetic to other members of the team. Isn't it interesting that so much of this work comes back to empathy and relationships? What norms do you have for your school or district? Do they promote empathy and relationship building? Do you encourage teams to actively talk about and set norms?

Working with schools across the country, we have seen it all. Some schools have well-established norms, some districts have very formal norms photocopied and laminated on the walls (we don't recommend going this route, as they are seen as fixed and unlikely to represent the true working nature of the group), and others have none. There is no one way to establish these as long as you remember that norms are organic, changing as the group grows and learns together. The creation of norms is the simple part; they can be created in a group brainstorm session. The much harder work comes with asking each member of the group to commit to living them. This means group members also commit to telling each other when they believe someone is violating an agreed-upon norm. The norms we bring as a starting place for the teams we work with (which you may use as a starting point if you need to create norms for a group) are:

- Assume best intentions.
- Be a learner, not a knower.
- Bring your authentic self.
- Take risks and choose to engage.
- Respect confidentiality.
- Play (and work) hard.

Norms are an indicator of success and can help a team navigate challenges. When conflict comes, and it always does, a winning team is able to handle the conflict with mutual respect and empathy for each other. Periodically evaluate the effectiveness of the team in achieving its goals and revisit the norms, asking if they are still the working norms of the group. If not, modify.

Adding New Members to Your Team—Hiring

Having the opportunity to add new members to your team is quite a luxury and provides a chance to round out the expertise of the team. Too often in education, we get stuck in the trap of hiring more of the same. This is natural; as humans, we yearn to be with people like us. However, when hiring, it is important to look for others, not for another. Today, more than ever, we need to be hiring people with the capability to learn, unlearn, and relearn. If you hire someone today for what they know, five years from now, they might be a liability. But if you hire them for their ability to learn, they are an asset. Assessing that quality can be tricky in an interview.

While working on really pushing the boundaries of what we could accomplish as a public school system, we quickly saw what an incredible opportunity it would be to rethink our hiring process. Somehow, over the years, our process had become fairly traditional, asking applicants to share textbook answers in front of a very formal interview panel. We were still experiencing success, but much like students learn to play the game of school, applicants learn to play the game of interviews. We became really intrigued with figuring out how to change the process. Being located near Silicon Valley, we tapped our parent community—many of whom worked for innovative companies such as Google, Facebook, LinkedIn, and Twitter—to ask for their expertise. How might they help us reimagine the hiring process? Based on research and parental input, we eliminated some of our more traditional questions and asked questions designed to elicit insights into a person's ability to think and act creatively. Some examples:

- "Tell us about a time when you created a new lesson, process, or program that was considered risky."
- "Tell us about a situation in which you had to come up with several new ideas in a hurry. Were they accepted? Were they successful?"
- "Tell us about one of your greatest failures and what you learned from it."
- "Engage us in a topic of your choosing for three minutes."

Sure, we still asked about differentiation and supporting the needs of students, but adding these more open-ended questions allowed us to assess applicants' ability to think, their ability to learn from failure, their risk tolerance, and their authenticity as a person. All these elements were important to us as we built our team to push the boundaries in learning. Do the questions you ask during interviews reflect the traits and characteristics that are most important to you in new hires? If not, how might you change them?

Broaden Your Team, Establish Purpose and Protocols

In Los Altos, we were focused on "revolutionizing learning for all students," a process that had consumed us for the better part of four years, although somewhere along our journey we realized we had been focused primarily on those who had direct interactions with students. We worked extensively with school leaders and even the parent community, but we had completely left out our support staff. Anyone who has worked in a school district knows how many people it takes behind the scenes at a school and a district to provide world-class education to students. How were we incorporating support staff in our work? We realized that some of the exciting changes that were happening at the classroom level and school level were having an impact at the district level. There were new and different strains on the system, yet we hadn't prepared people for the new strains. For example, we might have worked with teachers and principals on the importance of creating flexible learning environments, but we didn't bring our facilities departments into the same discussions. Our director of facilities was less than pleased to have many teachers calling and asking to have their desks removed, without any idea of why this request was coming. You can see how the lack of preparation on our part put the facilities department in an awkward situation. After a few run-ins, we recognized we had work to do. We experienced firsthand the need to include everyone in our process and also saw an opportunity to make commitments at the district level about the type of service we would provide to our school sites and to one another. Through this work, we got very explicit about our purpose and our commitments. We identified our purpose as follows: *To ensure the best learning experience possible is available each and every day for our students in their classrooms.*

Then, at the district office level, we decided the only way we would accomplish this was by working to give community members, parents, teachers, principals, and other staff what they need, when they needed it, with superior service. We would achieve this by keeping the operating protocols below at the forefront of our work each day, in every interaction.

Operating Protocols

Make It Easy

Focus on the needs of others and take the extra steps to ensure they feel supported.

- How will I make each interaction as easy as possible for others (placing any extra burden on me and not on them)?
- What will I do to make each person leave feeling supported and valued (happy/satisfied) during the interaction and at the conclusion?

Seek to Improve

Be open to ideas—seek and embrace change.

- How will I find ways to be more effective not only in my role, but also in other areas in the organization?
- How will I prepare to problem solve?
- How will I think ahead to prevent small issues from becoming large issues?
- How will I deal with an issue that requires additional time to resolve or is not in my area of expertise?

Assume Good Intentions

Work collaboratively, respecting and valuing what each person brings to the conversation.

- What is my mindset when asked for assistance?
- How will I exceed expectations in every interaction?
- How will I hold myself and others accountable for exemplary performance?
- How will my positive actions with others leave them feeling they have received superior service?
- Am I treating others the way I would expect to be treated as a customer/colleague?

While the purpose and operating protocols look quite simple, there was a lot of work that went into their creation. The protocols were commitments that we took seriously, so much so that the superintendent shared them publicly and asked people to contact him directly if they had an experience that did not align with the operating protocols. On the flip side, he also asked people to share if they had an experience that knocked their socks off.

This is only one example of how to broaden your team. What would it look like at your school or district? How will you ensure support staff are an integral part of the process?

Capacity Building and Diversity

The Justice League, a fictional superhero team appearing in American comic books, originally had seven members: Batman, Aquaman, the Flash, Green Lantern, Martian Manhunter, Superman, and Wonder Woman. What makes the Justice League so powerful is that each member has their own unique superpower. The Flash has superhuman speed. Superman can fly and has X-ray vision, among other powers. Wonder Woman is a skilled warrior, with Amazon bracelets and a golden lasso. You get the idea. These superheroes are powerful on their own, but the collective power of the Justice League is amazing! What are the superpowers on your team? And equally as important: what is everyone's kryptonite?

Whenever we have the opportunity to work with school teams, we like to begin our work by having individuals claim their superpower in a group, identify their kryptonite—essentially what brings them down in a group or kills their superpower—and share a recent accomplishment. A lot of times we are working with intact teams whose members have known each other for years, and yet every time there seems to be surprises. If we don't take the time to explicitly share our superpowers, how can we utilize them? Even if you don't take the time to do this as a group, you can start to identify the superpowers on your team by watching people in action and asking questions. "What do they do better than anything else? What do they do better than the people around them? What do they do without effort? What do they gravitate to without being asked?"

Identifying the superpowers on your team not only helps you build a stronger team, it can also help you connect people to opportunities and establish the right level of support for them. Our colleague Donna experienced this firsthand with Mary, a library media specialist in her district. Mary was discouraged with her role and even considering retirement. She has the ability to lead and inspire others, but was being dragged down by her kryptonite of meaningless work. She felt stuck. Because Donna took the time to know both Mary's superpowers and her kryptonite, she was able to connect her to a group of librarians rethinking libraries as the design hubs and makerspaces of the schools. Mary was reinvigorated and excited to dig into a new project. Not only is this team doing incredible work within the district, but Mary and her team are now presenting at conferences and talking to other librarians about reimagining the library spaces that exist on every school campus. What opportunities might you be able to connect your team to if you take the time to get to know their superpowers?

Opportunities and Support

Connecting team members to both opportunities and support is essential to the sustainability of your team. As a working parent, Alyssa is always looking for ways to streamline life, so imagine her excitement when she heard about Google Express, a shopping service from Google that will stop at up to three stores for you. From the comfort of her office in a matter of minutes, she ordered what she needed from Target, Costco, and CVS. When she got home that evening from work, her shopping from all three stores was sitting on her porch packaged in bags, each with a sticker that read, "Delivering you more free time." She was ecstatic! To have someone help with those errands freed her up to spend more time with her kids and family. How can we provide teachers and staff with more free time? Wouldn't it be amazing to provide teachers with tools and supports that freed up their time to do the really important work? This would be powerful at all levels of schools and districts.

The District of Columbia Public Schools are taking a lead in trying to "free the school principal" by adding directors of operations and logistics. The idea is to provide support for principals on daily issues that have little to do directly with teaching and learning: school maintenance, the cafeteria, safety, transportation, and paperwork. The goal is to liberate principals to focus more on teaching, evaluation of programs and personnel, future planning, and assessment. What would it look like to "free the teachers"? If we are going to be successful in asking our staffs to engage in new work, we might have to provide the space to do the work. Sometimes, that means helping them with the equivalent of running errands so they can engage in more meaningful work. Leaders who recognize this are getting creative in "delivering teachers more free time." One of the schools we visited created a parent volunteer copy squad, so teachers never have to spend their prep time doing clerical tasks. Let's support teachers when necessary through change to ease some of the burden. As soon as teachers see positive outcomes from their efforts, no matter how small, it's cathartic.

Moving in New Directions

Coming together is a beginning. Keeping together is progress.
Working together is success.

—Henry Ford, American captain of industry

With a broad team in place, you are ready to start moving them in new directions. Use the design-thinking process, but remember, it is just that: a process. Think of it as a suggestion, like a recipe you use the first time you cook a new dish, but don't let it limit you. Design-inspired leadership frees you from having all the answers all the time. Engage your team members in helping you identify where to start. Activate thinking using the three most powerful words, when combined: "How might we . . . ?" These three words are so powerful because the "how" implies there is not yet an answer and there is room for discovery, the "might" implies there is a world of possibility, and the "we" implies we are in this together. "How might we . . . ?" becomes an irresistible invitation to the work. Once people accept your invitation, you can continually nudge them further.

- *Move the goalposts a little at a time.* When we are looking to stretch beyond what we know, it helps if we move the endpoints a little at a time. Give your teams a chance to experience a series of small successes, building creative confidence, and then move to a larger scope. Think about learning to ride a bike. Most start with training wheels, then riding freely between adults, and finally making it solo to the end of the block. Once we get it, we're free to ride that bike in any direction. T.J. Edwards, director of design and engineering programs at Mt. Vernon, shared that change in education can feel like pushing against an ocean at times. To combat this, Mt. Vernon started using the word "ooooch," which they discovered in the book *Decisive,* by Chip Heath and Dan Heath. How can you "ooooch" closer to your goal? In posing this question, you are essentially asking people to think about small hacks they can make that can incrementally change experiences and policies. As a result, faculty tried "unschool" for one week a year, during which they had no bells and no classes, and students were allowed to work on passion projects. Unschool wasn't the goal; it was a little hack that eventually evolved into iProject. Now there are 90 minutes a week when students can work on passion projects in school. It is oversimplifying to say that the "unschool experience" led right to iProject, but it was definitely instrumental in changing people's thinking. Incremental changes, combined with effective storytelling, are key as you move closer to the goal.

• *Ask for harder work, not more work.* At times, it feels as if we leave our team meetings with a longer to-do list, thinking that if we were just able to get more done before the next meeting, we could be finished. Perhaps the work that we need to be helping our teams do is deeper and more thoughtful. If we focused on a specific practice, such as homework, and armed team members with a list of thoughtful questions to examine through their own individual practices, the discussions that they would come back to would be very different than if we asked them to just bring in homework samples and policies for a surface comparison and a debate of who does it better. Asking teachers to dig into their beliefs and values allows a much deeper and more thoughtful conversation, which leads to a consensus with a better understanding of needed changes. Get comfortable asking other people to be uncomfortable. Learning comes from discomfort.

- *Use assessment as proof.* Educators are driven by data, so include ways to show early on that change is working. Assessment comes in many shapes and sizes. Think about ways to gather and engage with feedback, using different formative assessment measures. Also, build in some more formal assessment methods: surveys, interviews, student artifacts of learning, testimonials, and other data points that support your initiative. When you are ready to analyze your first prototype, think about what proof you want brought to the table. You might start with those quick formative assessments and build into more formal and in-depth forms of proof as you work toward a final version. Figure 8.1 is an example of a self-assessment that we used with our team of principals. As a district, we had been working on a number of initiatives, such as personalizing learning, providing meaningful professional development to teachers, creating school climates that promote creativity and innovation, and active learning spaces. This simple rubric allowed school principals to acknowledge where their staff was on each of the initiatives, and we were able to have a powerful conversation as a result.

Creating a Network

Building your team is so much bigger than just the people at your school or in your district. The same people sitting around the same table produce the same results. To avoid this sameness trap, you have to create a network and find kindred spirits outside your organization who can provide both inspiration and support. These kindred spirits can help push your thinking and see what is possible in different contexts with different constraints.

Figure 8.1

Assessment Rubric on Change Initiatives

	Not on My Radar	Mulling It Over	Sporadic Implementation	Everyone's on Board
Personalize learning for every student	Heard about it, but that's it.	I understand the concept and have had discussions with staff about it.	Some of the teachers at my school are implementing strategies to achieve this.	Every classroom has at least one strategy in place that tries to meet this goal.
Access to meaningful professional development	We have professional development available.	I am discussing with my staff the iLearn opportunities and instructional coach support that is available.	A decent number of my teachers are taking advantage of the professional development opportunities.	Why don't you just offer the professional development classes at my school site since all our teachers attend?
Create school climates that promote creativity and innovation	Are #2 pencils innovative?	My staff is curious and beginning to question how they might innovate in their classrooms.	There are strong pockets of creativity and innovation around my campus.	My staff is all pulling in the same direction and working together to develop creative and innovative opportunities for kids.

	Not on My Radar	Mulling It Over	Sporadic Implementation	Everyone's on Board
Active learning spaces	Desks, chairs, rows.	I have seen some interesting examples of active learning spaces and would like to know more.	A few of my classrooms have actually reorganized their "teaching space" and now think of it as "learning space."	I have many teachers asking me about furniture and space and how they can improve the learning spaces for students.
Access to technology that encourages meaningful collaboration	We have walkie-talkies in the office.	I have heard about that Twitter thing.	I have a handful of teachers using electronic tools to collaborate with students and colleagues.	I could hold my staff meeting using Edmodo! In fact, I am not sure I need to be there.

Kindred spirits can be found in many different places. Through social media, we have discovered new friends and educators who are striving for some of the same educational changes. Try using a hashtag—#edleadership, #changeschool, or #dtk12—in a Twitter search. You will find Tweets from others who are interested in the topics you can follow. Look for Twitter chats, such as #dtk12chat or #edchat, and participate in conversations. Conferences can also offer a great place to find your people. While sessions are great places to learn, look for makerspaces and blogger's cafes where you can sit and interact with other conference attendees.

Part of creating a network is to act as the connector and intentionally bring people together. Mt. Vernon Presbyterian School in Atlanta, Georgia, has mastered the art of networking and connecting within their community. In 2013, Mt. Vernon launched a Council on Innovation, bringing together 18 individuals who are experts in entrepreneurship, education, business, and community leadership. Members included leaders from Coca-Cola, Turner Entertainment, Spanx, The Weather Channel, and many other businesses vital to Atlanta. This council was established to provide insight and inspiration to the school's leadership team. Mt. Vernon's leadership poses questions to the council, such as, "How might we continue to prepare our students to be globally competitive?" "How might we connect our students to authentic learning opportunities in the community?" Through the Council on Innovation, Mt. Vernon has been able to identify what it means to be globally competitive and ground this work in the community. How might you leverage your community to create a network of learning for the school?

Go Flat

We often hear the words "top down" or "flat" as a way to describe an organization. Top down implies that all decisions filter down from the top, and those at the bottom are powerless. To flatten an organization means that leadership decisions are spread across all stakeholders and everyone is part of the process. Education has traditionally relied on a top-down model, and most educational institutions embrace this structure. This top-down leadership structure can be detrimental to our teacher leaders. Often they become burned out and leave the classroom, looking for an opportunity to have a bigger impact. Sometimes this leads to administration, one of the only options in the education world for higher salaries and more global responsibilities. Teachers are our greatest assets. How might we empower teacher leadership roles so that they feel valuable and have a wider impact? Moving from a top-down organization to one that is flat is challenging; however, it is a vital move for education. We need to find a way to use the many talents that are spread across our school sites in ways that encourage and value each individual. And even if we may not be able to "go flat," at the very least we need to commit to models of distributed leadership in our schools and establish teacher leaders who have responsibilities beyond their classroom. At Design39 in Poway, teachers are empowered to make many of the decisions. They have distributed leadership through a multi-team approach. Teachers meet as a grade-level team to design learning experiences and discuss school issues, and also as multi-grade-level spans to compare and discuss alignment. They then meet as a whole group with their principal to bring all discussions together and strive for consensus over major decisions. While they are still working through some of their meeting protocols and processes, they feel that every staff member has an opportunity to express their views in the decision-making process.

A Final Word Before You Begin: Design Your Mindset

It always seems impossible until it's done!

—Nelson Mandela

Throughout this book, "change" is a major player. No surprise, and not really new news. There are tons of articles out there about how hard change is, tips for how to manage change, and motivational pieces to help see you through change in an organization. In fact, if you Google "change is hard," there are 123,000,000 results. We haven't taken the time to investigate all these resources, but the sheer number of related items is a clear indicator that change is something humanity struggles with. Now, this isn't to discount all the incredible research that has been done on the difficulty of change. Clearly there is a lot to be learned about change. But what if we were able to reframe change from "being hard" to "being messy"? This simple alteration of word choice has helped us rethink a lot of ideas about change.

Reframing change from "hard" to "messy" instantly makes it feel more doable and action-oriented. We all have different tolerance levels of messiness, but we all know what it feels like to be in the middle of a mess. In our chaotic world of change, some form of messiness comes with the day-to-day. Two things we have learned: some of the best times come from the biggest messes. Watching children come home with dirt caked on their clothes and under their fingernails means it was a good day at school. The other thing we have learned is that messes are temporary. All messes eventually get cleaned up. Embracing the messiness of change seems to give permission to experiment and freedom to play and investigate answers along the way. How many people have we let off the hook by overstating how hard change is, thereby giving them permission not to change? It is our hope that we collectively embrace the messiness of change and get going!

So where do you start? Our advice is to start where you are and start with whatever problem is in front of you. There is no perfect solution or prescription; it really is about engaging with the problems you face using new design-inspired mindsets and skills. As you engage in the messiness of the work, we offer a few final thoughts.

Be You

Channel your inner Oprah and be authentic. During Oprah's first nationally syndicated shows airing in 1986, Oprah shared with the audience that she had hives in her armpits from being so nervous. Jesse Jackson told Oprah she is the only person he has ever met who is exactly the same way she is off television as she is on. That is a huge compliment and perhaps one of the reasons that Oprah has gone on to be one of the most influential women in the world. While we don't expect you to talk about hives in your armpits, think about your own signature presence. What makes you unique as a leader? Own it and bring it to the table.

Run Your Own Race

We have shared stories of amazing leaders, schools, and districts. It can be easy to get caught up in comparing yourself, your school, or your district to those shared; however, the more time you spend comparing yourself to what others are doing, the less time you are focusing on your situation and your own success. Think back to the beloved story of the tortoise and the hare. The hare was speeding for success, but got caught in his own arrogance and simply coasted. Meanwhile, the tortoise plodded down his path, one step at a time. Every school or organization has a unique set of circumstances. You can only practice leading like a designer in the circumstances you are in. Unlike the tortoise and the hare, there is no need to focus on winning the race. The challenge is to just be more like the tortoise, intentionally moving toward the finish line.

Practice Gratitude

We are so fortunate to do the work we do; there is nothing more powerful than impacting the lives of future generations.

Take a moment to reflect and remember this. Gratitude sees what is good and right with the world. Gratitude can help us find something meaningful in nothing. Leaders who see their staff through the lens of gratitude will always see the untapped potential in people and inspire them to achieve what others think is impossible.

Be Passionate

Passionate leaders spread passion to others through their love of the work, doing new things, taking risks, being motivated, having a sense of urgency, and reinventing themselves. The more passionate you are about the work, the more likely you are to awaken possibility within others. Challenge yourself to notice the number of shining eyes you have around you. How might you involve other people in your passion rather than go it alone?

Together, we explored the changing landscape of leadership and explored five practical ways to reframe the school leader role using design. Our hope is that through this journey, you will start to see your world differently and bring a new perspective to your work. We hope you now see yourself as a designer, capable of inspiring great change and addressing challenges with new insights and methods. While the tools and strategies we have shared are powerful accelerators of change, none of them matter if the thinking doesn't change. Shift thinking first, then anything is possible. The more you adopt the mindset and realize it's not about following a prescription, the more successful you will be. As a design-inspired leader, you are at the forefront of a new movement in education, one that will move traditional education into the modern world and drive the future of learning.

Appendix

Tips for Empathy Interviews

- *Ask why.* Even when you think you know the answer, try asking people why they do or say the things they do; sometimes the answers will surprise you. Unlike other interviews, empathy interviews don't require a lot of questions. Let the responses flow.
- *Avoid "usually," "always,"and "rarely."* Instead, try to ask about a specific instance or occurrence, for example, "Tell me about the last time you _____."
- *Encourage stories.* Whether or not the stories people tell are true, stories reveal how people think about the world and the topics you are discussing.
- *Pay attention to nonverbal cues.* Watch facial expressions and body language.
- *Listen for inconsistencies.* Sometimes what people say they do and what they actually do are different. Interesting insights can be hidden here.
- *Allow for silence.* Interviewers often feel the need to ask another question if there is any silence; resist this urge and practice your best wait time. Some of the deeper responses come after a moment of thought and reflection.
- *Position questions neutrally.* "What was the last powerful professional learning experience you participated in?" is a

better question than "Don't you think all professional learning experiences need to be revamped?" because the first question doesn't imply that there is a correct answer.

- *Avoid binary questions.* Binary questions can be answered in one word; remember, you are trying to host a conversation that is built on stories.

Empathy Interview Format

- *Introduction.* Introduce yourself and your partner. Tell them what you are doing. ("We're trying to learn more about the parent experience at our school.")
- *Kickoff.* Shift the focus from you to them. Ask their names and any other pertinent general information.
- *Specific questions.* Use questions drafted prior to the interview that are specific to your topic, but don't be afraid to go in unexpected directions.
- *Prompts to get unstuck.* Don't be afraid of some silence, but prepare additional questions to encourage elaboration if the stories aren't flowing in the course of the interview, such as, "Why?" "Why did you do/say/think that?" "Really? And why was that?" "Can you say more about that?" "Tell me more."
- *Last chance.* Signal that the interview is over, but keep listening! Sometimes interviewees offer the most interesting information as they are walking out the door.

Turn a "Yeah, But..." into a "Yes, And..."

- *Dare to imagine.* What is the biggest difference you could make? What would learning look like if you had no constraints? Spend some time in the world of possibility.
- *Yeah, but . . . .* Identify all the reasons you can't accomplish the goals you listed above. Be specific. What is the reason and whom is it coming from? There may be different constraints coming from teachers, community, the union, and the school board.
- *Use constraints to your advantage.* For every "yeah, but . . ." listed, brainstorm three ways to navigate around or use the constraint to your advantage.
- *Simple change = profound impact.* What is the simplest thing you can do that will have the most profound impact and move you closer to your goal? Is there something small, like a practice or rule, that is getting in your way? If so, investigate it using a simple one-two-three approach:

    1. Identify (one simple rule or practice getting in your way).

    2. Ask why (the rule or practice exists).

    3. Modify (the rule or practice to make a big impact).

- *Yes, and . . . .* Share the work you have done in the above steps with faculty, community members, or even the school board. Invite them to explore your imagined better version, the very real constraints, and possible solutions. Once they have the lay of the land, invite them to add on to your possible solutions with a simple "yes, and . . . ."

Experience Design Planning Template

- *Who is involved in this experience?* The more specific you can be, the better. In fact, if you can identify how the users think, you can start to empathize with their needs.
- *Why is this experience taking place?* Why are people taking part in this experience? What are their end goals, and what do they hope to achieve?
- *What options are available?* Challenge your own assumptions about the experience you are planning and play with lots of ideas before settling on the ones you will execute.
- *Where is this experience taking place (or where would it be best for this experience to take place)?* Is it happening at school, in the teachers' lounge, or in a setting outside of school?

How to Plan an Outstanding Experience

- Identify the users.
- Establish your "why."
- Select the location.
- Set the stage (details matter).
  —Prework
  —Music
  —Snacks
- Make it meaningful.
  —What's the "how"?
- Allow for choice.
- Remember the fun factor.
- Wrap it up.
  —What's next?
  —Reflection

Rapid Prototyping and Testing Process and Materials Checklist

❑ *Start simply*. The most successful prototypes are those that are developed early in a process. They actually invite users to contribute to your learning process and design with you.

❑ *Figure out the story you want to tell about your idea*. Using as few words as possible, what is the best way to convey your thinking? Select a prototype form (sketchnotes, role-play, physical model) that communicates the essence of your idea or solution.

❑ *Show, don't tell*. Use pictures, create artifacts, or introduce role-plays. Try to engage your users with a prototype that speaks for itself.

❑ *Ask for feedback*. Share your ideas directly with your end users, asking for feedback with generative prompts such as "I like...," "I wish...," and "What if...?" Resist the urge to defend your thinking; be gracious and thank the users for their feedback.

❑ *Integrate feedback and iterate*. How can you incorporate the feedback you received? Make changes to your prototype and get back out there. Build and test to learn.

❑ *Play with your prototypes*. Remember, you are building to learn and want honest feedback, even if it contradicts your ideas. Keeping a playful spirit with prototyping can help you be more open to any feedback you receive.

Prototyping Corner Materials

A prototype can be made with anything, but to get started, it is helpful to gather materials. Once your prototyping corner is set up, you'll be surprised how easy it becomes to add to these materials.

- Cardboard
- Paper (any color, size, shape)
- Paper plates
- Tape (Scotch tape, duct tape, masking tape)
- Recycled materials
- Stapler
- Paper clips
- Markers, crayons, colored pencils
- Glue (glue sticks, hot glue gun)
- Pipe cleaners
- Aluminum foil, wax paper
- Popsicle sticks, toothpicks

Conducting a Story Audit

- *Define your intention.* If you could write any story about your district, school, or classroom, what would it be? Know what your story should sound like, feel like, and look like.
- *Walk it.* Take a purposeful walk through your learning spaces.
  —What artifacts line the walls?
  —What evidence of learning do you see? Can you see process or just product? Is student thinking visible?
  —What signs are on your campus? Do they encourage a positive culture?
  —Is your vision evident on the walk?
- *Talk it.* As you take your walk, stop and ask for stories.
  —Ask students to tell you what they're learning.
  —Ask teachers to tell you a story about the lesson they just taught.
  —Ask a parent to tell you a story about their child at your school.
  —Are these stories reflective of the culture you are building?

A Hero's Journey: The Leaders' Version

What story do you want to tell and where are you in the journey?
Try the following story frame:

We currently [*action or practice that you're looking to change*],
but we would like to [*your new idea*]. This would be amazing
because [*clearly define your vision pitch, grounded in your why*].
In order to begin, we will need [*who or what*] and [*a plan with an
architected experience*]. We will also need [*what might be some
obvious pain points that you can plan ahead for? what rules might
you need to intentionally break?*]. When or if some things fall
apart, we will [*what life preservers might you need? what plan for
recovery?*]. Our best storytellers are [*how might you effectively
tell the story of change?*]. We will celebrate wins and amplify the
good by [*how will you recognize, motivate, and celebrate?*] This
change will lead to [*how will things be different? where might you
go next?*].

Bibliography

Amaze your education colleagues. (n.d.). Retrieved from http://www.sciencegeek. net/lingo.html

Anaissie, T., Cary, V., Clifford, D., Malarkey, T., & Wise, S. (n.d.). Liberatory design cards. Retrieved from http://www.dschool.stanford.edu/resources/liberato-ry-design-cards

Austin, C. (2014). These six companies broke the rules of business . . . and suc-ceeded. *HuffPost*. Retrieved from http://www.huffingtonpost.com/2014/09/24/ successful-businesses-breaking-rules_n_5767894.html

Barnes, M., & Gonzalez, J. (2015). *Hacking education: 10 quick fixes for every school*. Cleveland, OH: Times 10 Publications.

Barrett, T. (2016). Applying design thinking in 4 different ways in schools. *Medium*. Retrieved from http://medium.com/@tombarrett/applying-design-think-ing-in-4-different-ways-in-schools-9ab7c9dd6826#.6hwdxwm4m

Bonchek, M. (2016). Why the problem with learning is unlearning. *Harvard Business Review*. Retrieved from http://hbr.org/2016/11/why-the-problem-with-learning-is-unlearning

Booher, D. (2015). 7 tips for great storytelling as a leader. *Fast Company*. Retrieved from http://www.fastcompany.com/3040709/7-tips-for-great-storytelling-as-a-leader

Brignull, H. (2016). How to run an empathy & user journey mapping workshop. *Medium*. Retrieved from http://medium.com/@harrybr/how-to-run-an-empa-thy-user-journey-mapping-workshop-813f3737067

Brown, T. & Katz, B. (2011). *Change by design: How design thinking transforms organizations and inspires innovation*. New York: HarperCollins.

Businessballs. (n.d.). Mehrabian's communication theory—Verbal, non-verbal, body language. Retrieved from http://www.businessballs.com/mehrabian-communications.htm

Busse, S. (2012). How spilt coffee created a billion dollar mop. *Kinesis.* Retrieved from http://www.kinesisinc.com/how-spilt-coffee-created-a-billion-dollar-mop/

Carpenter, D. (2016). Why people who break the rules have higher incomes. *ITX Design.* Retrieved from http://www.itxdesign.com/why-people-who-break-the-rules-have-higher-incomes/

Collins English Dictionary. (n.d.). Definition of 'empathy.' Retrieved from https://www.collinsdictionary.com/us/dictionary/english/empathy

Consumer Reports. (2016). What your web browser says about you. Retrieved from http://www.consumerreports.org/computers/what-your-web-browser-says-about-you

Cuddy, A. J. C., Kohut, M., & Neffinger, J. (2013). Connect, then lead. *Harvard Business Review.* Retrieved from http://hbr.org/2013/07/connect-then-lead

De La Cruz, D. (2016). What kids wish their teachers knew. *The New York Times.* Retrieved from http://www.nytimes.com/2016/08/31/well/family/what-kids-wish-their-teachers-knew.html

Denning, P., & Dunham, R. (2012). *The innovator's way: Essential practices for successful innovation.* Cambridge, MA: The MIT Press.

Design Thinking. (n.d.). Thoughts by Tim Brown. Retrieved from https://design-thinking.ideo.com/?page_id=1542Â Â

DesMarais, C. (2015). 5 clues it's time to pivot. *Inc.* Retrieved from http://www.inc.com/christina-desmarais/5-clues-it-s-time-to-pivot.html

Duhigg, C. (2014). *The power of habit: Why we do what we do in life and business.* New York: Random House.

Duhigg, C. (2016). What Google learned from its quest to build the perfect team. *The New York Times.* Retrieved from http://www.nytimes.com/2016/02/28/magazine/what-google-learned-from-its-quest-to-build-the-perfect-team.html

Dyer, J. H., Gregersen, H. B., & Christensen, C. M. (2011). *The innovator's DNA: Mastering the five skills of disruptive innovators.* Boston: Harvard Business Press.

Empathy quiz. (n.d.). *Greater Good Magazine.* Retrieved from http://greatergood.berkeley.edu/quizzes/take_quiz/14

Ertel, C., & Solomon, L.K. (2014). *Moments of impact: How to design strategic conversations that accelerate change.* New York: Simon & Schuster.

Evans, L. (2014). 25 ways to ask your kids 'So how was school today?' without asking them 'So how was school today?' *HuffPost.* Retrieved from http://www.huffingtonpost.com/liz-evans/25-ways-to-ask-your-kids-so-how-was-school-today-without-asking-them-so-how-was-school-today_b_5738338.html

Fallon, N. (2014). Devil in the details: Startups must stay 'big-picture.' *Business News Daily.* Retrieved from http://www.businessnewsdaily.com/6172-how-to-see-big-picture.html

Folkman, J. (2011). 10 ways to pull, rather than push, for results. *Zenger Folkman*. Retrieved from http://zengerfolkman.com/10-ways-to-pull-rather-than-push-for-results

Friedberg, D. (2011). Recognizing opportunity in the rain. *Stanford eCorner*. Retrieved from https://ecorner.stanford.edu/in-brief/recognizing-opportunity-in-the-rain/

Gibbons, S. (2016). Design thinking builds strong teams. *Nielsen Norman Group*. Retrieved from http://www.nngroup.com/articles/design-thinking-team-building/

Giudice, M., & Ireland, C. (2014). *Rise of the DEO: Leadership by design*. Berkeley, CA: New Riders.

Goldring, R., & Taie, S. (2014). *Principal attrition and mobility: Results from the 2012–13 principal follow-up survey* (NCES 2014-064rev). U.S. Department of Education. Washington, DC: National Center for Education Statistics.

Goodreads. (n.d.). The end of average quotes. Retrieved from https://www.goodreads.com/work/quotes/44945876-the-end-of-average-how-we-succeed-in-a-wolrd-that-values-sameness

Goodwin, T. (2015). The battle is for the customer interface. *TechCrunch*. Retrieved from https://techcrunch.com/2015/03/03/in-the-age-of-disintermediation-the-battle-is-all-for-the-customer-interface/

Gotkin, Z. (2012). America's innovative companies are going flat. *HuffPost*. Retrieved from http://www.huffingtonpost.com/zev-gotkin/corporate-hierarchy-work_b_1962345.html

Grant, A. (2017). *Originals: How non-conformists move the world*. New York: Penguin Books.

Gray, A. (2016). The 10 skills you need to thrive in the Fourth Industrial Revolution. *World Economic Forum*. Retrieved from http://www.weforum.org/agenda/2016/01/the-10-skills-you-need-to-thrive-in-the-fourth-industrial-revolution/

Gray, D., Brown, S., & Macanufo, J. (2010). *Gamestorming: A playbook for innovators, rulebreakers, and changemakers*. Beijing, China: O'Reilly.

Heath, C., & Heath, D. (2013). *Decisive: How to make better choices in life and work*. New York: Currency.

Ibarra, H., & Hunter, M. L. (2007). How leaders create and use networks. *Harvard Business Review*. Retrieved from https://hbr.org/2007/01/how-leaders-create-and-use-networks

The Innovator's Way. (2010). The innovator's way: Essential practices for successful innovation. Retrieved from http://innovators-way.com/excerpts/#promise

itechgear. (2011). *Original iPod 1000 songs in your pocket by Steve Jobs* [Video file]. Retrieved from https://www.youtube.com/watch?v=6SUJNspeux8

Jones, J. (2012). The homeless man and the NYPD cop's boots: how a warm tale turns cold. *The Guardian*. Retrieved from http://www.theguardian.com/commentisfree/2012/dec/04/homeless-man-nypd-cop-boots

Kelley, T. (2005). The ten faces of innovation: Chapter 2: the experimenter. Retrieved from http://www.tenfacesofinnovation.com/tenfaces/index.htm

Kelley, T. (2008a). Field observations with fresh eyes [Video file]. *Stanford eCorner.* Retrieved from https://ecorner.stanford.edu/video/field-observations-with-fresh-eyes/

Kelley, T. (2008b). Thinking like a traveler [Video file]. *Stanford eCorner.* Retrieved from https://ecorner.stanford.edu/video/thinking-like-a-traveler/

Kelley, T., & Kelley, D. (2015). *Creative confidence: Unleashing the creative potential within us all.* London: William Collins.

Kelley, T., & Littman, J. (2005). *The ten faces of innovation: IDEO's strategies for beating the devil's advocate & driving creativity throughout your organization.* New York: Currency/Doubleday.

The KIND Foundation. (2017). The KIND Foundation launches social media experiment that challenges Americans to add different perspectives to their Facebook feeds. *PR Newswire.* Retrieved from http://www.prnewswire.com/news-releases/the-kind-foundation-launches-social-media-experiment-that-challenges-americans-to-add-different-perspectives-to-their-facebook-feeds-300440450.html

Konnikova, M. (2014). Multitask masters. *The New Yorker.* Retrieved from http://www.newyorker.com/science/maria-konnikova/multitask-masters

Liberson, G. (2011). Networking for innovation. *HuffPost.* Retrieved from http://www.huffingtonpost.com/gary-liberson/networking-for-innovation_b_926794.html

Lichtenberg, J., Woock, C., & Wright, M. (2008). Ready to innovate: Are educators and executives aligned on the creative readiness of the U.S. workforce? The Conference Board. Research report R-1424-08-RR. Retrieved from https://www.americansforthearts.org/sites/default/files/ReadytoInnovateFull.pdf

Light, N. (2017). This principal is not normal: A sofa office, glittery shoes and a trampoline make learning cool. *Dallas News.* Retrieved from http://www.dallasnews.com/news/education/2017/05/10/principal-normal-sofa-office-glittery-shoes-trampoline-make-learning-cool

Madson, P. R. (2005). *Improv wisdom: Don't prepare, just show up.* New York: Bell Tower.

Marketing-Schools.org. (2012a). Pull marketing. Retrieved from http://www.marketing-schools.org/types-of-marketing/pull-marketing.html

Marketing-Schools.org. (2012b). Push marketing. Retrieved from http://www.marketing-schools.org/types-of-marketing/push-marketing.html

Metro Bank. (n.d.). Our brief but brilliant history. Retrieved from http://www.metrobankonline.co.uk/about-us/

Moran, G. (2015). The rules to breaking the rules. *Fast Company.* Retrieved from http://www.fastcompany.com/3041327/the-rules-to-breaking-the-rules

Morgan, A., & Barden, M. (2015). *A beautiful constraint: how to transform your limitations into advantages, and why it's everyone's business.* Hoboken, NJ: Wiley.

Morgan, J. (2015). Why the future of work is all about the employee experience. *Forbes.* Retrieved from https://www.forbes.com/sites/jacobmorgan/2015/05/27/why-the-future-of-work-is-all-about-the-employee-experience/

Motionographer. (2017). What makes a good producer? Retried from http://motionographer.com/2017/01/30/what-makes-a-good-producer/

Patnaik, D., & Mortensen, P. (2009). *Wired to care: How companies prosper when they create widespread empathy.* Upper Saddle River, NJ: FT Press.

Raskin, A. (2017). Why leadership = storytelling. *The Mission.* Retrieved from http://medium.com/the-mission/why-leadership-equals-storytelling-71877abfe1f0

Rodale, M. (2016). The importance of networking (and how to do it well). *HuffPost.* Retrieved from http://www.huffingtonpost.com/maria-rodale/the-importance-of-network_b_9039062.html

Rose, T. (2016). *The end of average: How to succeed in a world that values sameness.* London: Allen Lane.

Rosenstein, J. (2014). 5 strategies for big-picture thinking. *Fast Company.* Retrieved from http://www.fastcompany.com/3036143/5-strategies-for-big-picture-thinking

Saxena, H. (2014). Managing the paradox of big picture & operational precision. *Ivey Business Journal.* Retrieved from http://www.iveybusinessjournal.com/publication/managing-the-paradox-of-big-picture-operational-precision/

Schwartz, K. (2016). *I wish my teacher knew: How one question can change everything for our kids.* Boston: Da Capo Lifelong Books.

Sebastian, D. (2016). What are elements of a great learning experience? *Smart Sparrow.* Retrieved from http://www.smartsparrow.com/2016/03/04/what-makes-a-learning-experience-great/

Seelig, T. (2013). How reframing a problem unlocks innovation. *Co.Design.* Retrieved from http://www.fastcodesign.com/1672354/how-reframing-a-problem-unlocks-innovation

Sinek, S. (2013). *Start with why: How great leaders inspire everyone to take action.* London: Portfolio/Penguin.

Skavlan. (2017). *Samuel West from the "Museum of Failure" showing some epic product fails* [Video file]. Retrieved from https://www.youtube.com/watch?v=eBtXNPy3hic

Smart Design. (n.d.). Getting a grip: A longtime partnership that changed kitchens everywhere. Retrieved from http://smartdesignworldwide.com/projects/oxo-partnership/

Solis, B. (2015). What makes a truly great experience? Retrieved from http://www.briansolis.com/2015/11/makes-truly-great-experience/

Solomon, L. K. (2015). The real winners of the Oscars (and what it tells us about innovation). *Medium.* Retrieved from http://www.medium.com/@lisakaysolomon/and-the-oscar-goes-to-innovation-1670b2329357

Solomon, L.K. (2015). The rise of the producer. *Medium*. Retrieved from http://lisakaysolomon.com/2015/10/27/the-rise-of-the-producer/

Spool, J. M. (2017). The power of experience mapping. *UX Immersion: Interactions*. Retrieved from http://www.medium.com/ux-immersion-interactions/the-power-of-experience-mapping-212ba81e5ee

Spool, J. M. (n.d.). Design is the rendering of intent. *UIE: Articles*. Retrieved from https://articles.uie.com/design_rendering_intent/

Thieda, K. (2014). Brené Brown on empathy vs. sympathy. *Psychology Today*. Retrieved from http://www.psychologytoday.com/blog/partnering-in-mental-health/201408/bren-brown-empathy-vs-sympathy-0

Top 6 rules that every student wants to break in school. (2015). *India Today*. Retrieved from https://www.indiatoday.in/education-today/featurephilia/story/top-6-rules-that-every-student-wants-to-break-in-school-240652-2015-02-17

Usborne, D. (2012). The moment it all went wrong for Kodak. *The Independent*. Retrieved from http://www.independent.co.uk/news/business/analysis-and-features/the-moment-it-all-went-wrong-for-kodak-6292212.html

Valve. (n.d.). Our people. Retrieved from http://www.valvesoftware.com/company/people.html

Walker, R. (2014). How to pay attention: 20 ways to win the war against seeing. *re:form*. Retrieved from http://medium.com/re-form/how-to-pay-attention-4751adb53cb6

West, H. (2014). A chain of innovation: The creation of Swiffer: Thinking about the many stories that contribute to a successful innovation can add depth and perspective to our understanding of how innovation happens. *Research-Technology Management*. Retrieved from http://www.questia.com/library/journal/1G1-367076982/a-chain-of-innovation-the-creation-of-swiffer-thinking

Wicked problem. (n.d.). *Wikipedia*. Retrieved August 9, 2017, from https://en.wikipedia.org/wiki/Wicked_problem

Wiseman, L., Allen, L., & Foster, E. (2013). *The multiplier effect: Tapping the genius inside our schools*. Thousand Oaks, CA: Corwin.

World Economic Forum. (2016a). *The future of jobs*. Retrieved from http://reports.weforum.org/future-of-jobs-2016/

World Economic Forum. (2016b). *The future of jobs: Employment, skills and workforce strategy for the fourth industrial revolution*. Retrieved from http://www3.weforum.org/docs/WEF_FOJ_Executive_Summary_Jobs.pdf

World Economic Forum. (2016c). *The future of jobs: Employment, skills and workforce strategy for the fourth industrial revolution*. Retrieved from http://www3.weforum.org/docs/WEF_Future_of_Jobs.pdf

X, the moonshot factory. (2013). *What is moonshot thinking?* [Video file]. Retrieved from https://www.youtube.com/watch?v=0uaquGZKx_0

Index

The letter *f* following a page number denotes a figure.

About the Authors

 **Alyssa Gallagher** is an experienced public school educator, school and district administrator, facilitator, and educational consultant. She has successfully led districtwide blended learning initiatives, helped schools create integrated STEM programs, and launched strategic plans using Design Thinking. Having worked in a variety of roles—from school principal to assistant superintendent of schools—Gallagher understands firsthand the complexity of educational leadership and is passionate about improving the learning experiences created in schools. She is constantly exploring "What if. . .?" with school leaders and works to support radical change in education.

 **Kami Thordarson** has worked in many roles as a public educator—from classroom teacher to professional development and curriculum designer. She enjoys engaging students and teachers with learning experiences that focus on authenticity and relevance. Thordarson is involved with the Design Thinking movement in K–12 education and, in her current role as an administrator, works to lead a district in integrating technology into learning and innovating practices that fully move students into more personalized experiences. She values

the challenge of helping school leaders develop real-world classrooms where teachers facilitate and lead students through work that empowers them to make an impact on the world.

Gallagher and Thordarson are widely recognized experts on Design Thinking, educational leadership, and innovative strategies that reflect 21st century learners whose message resonates well in the field. They train, speak, and lead workshops with educators all over the United States, having shared their expertise in over 10 states as well as Denmark and Germany. They have been invited to share their leadership strategies with several districts throughout California with participants who have attended conference sessions. They are frequent presenters at ASCD, ISTE, SXSWedu, ACSA, and CUE, and have been published in ASCD's *Education Update* and featured in Liz Wiseman's *The Multiplier Effect,* Salman Khan's *The One-Room Schoolhouse: Education Reimagined,* and Grant Lichtman's *#EdJourney: A Roadmap to the Future of Education.*

WHOLE CHILD
TENETS

The ASCD Whole Child approach is an effort to transition from a focus on narrowly defined academic achievement to one that promotes the long-term development and success of all children. Through this approach, ASCD supports educators, families, community members, and policymakers as they move from a vision about educating the whole child to sustainable, collaborative actions.

Design Thinking for School Leaders relates to the **engaged, supported**, and **challenged** tenets. *For more about the ASCD Whole Child approach, visit **www.ascd.org/wholechild.***

1 HEALTHY
Each student enters school healthy and learns about and practices a healthy lifestyle.

2 SAFE
Each student learns in an environment that is physically and emotionally safe for students and adults.

3 ENGAGED
Each student is actively engaged in learning and is connected to the school and broader community.

4 SUPPORTED
Each student has access to personalized learning and is supported by qualified, caring adults.

5 CHALLENGED
Each student is challenged academically and prepared for success in college or further study and for employment and participation in a global environment.

LEARN. TEACH. LEAD.